STICKMEN'S GUIDE TO HOW THINGS WORK

by John Farndon
Illustrated by John Paul

BEETLE BOOKS

Beetle Books is a
Hungry Tomato imprint

First published in 2020
by Hungry Tomato Ltd
F1, Old Bakery Studios
Blewetts Wharf, Malpas Road
Truro, TR1 1QH, UK
Copyright © 2020 Hungry Tomato Ltd

A CIP catalog record for this book is
available from the British Library.

ISBN 978-1-913077-167

Printed and bound in China

Discover more at
www.mybeetlebooks.com

Contents

How Things Work

Two centuries ago, the only way to get around on land was to plod along on legs—two (walking) or four (horseback). Nowadays, billions of cars, motorcycles, trains, ships, and watercraft whisk us quickly everywhere we need to go. And we are completely surrounded by machines—some of which are truly monstrous in size. Join the Stickmen as they discover how all of this works...

The Long Road

The world's roads stretch for 40 million miles, with about a tenth (4 million miles) in the USA—the most roads of any country.

Rail Passengers

Around the world, passengers travel a total of 1.8 trillion miles every year on the railroads. Very little of that rail travel is in the US, though, where the car is king. The real railroad fans are in India, where people travel half a trillion miles by rail every year. If you go to India, you'll see that they have to really crowd in to get on a train, with people often sitting on the roof in rush hours.

Cruising from Miami

To go on an ocean cruise, the Port of Miami is the place to be. Miami is the cruise capital of the world with over 4 million passengers leaving for a trip on the ocean every year. There are eight passenger terminals here for ocean-going cruise ships, and all are constantly busy.

Underwater World

Somewhere under the sea right now, dozens of nuclear submarines are moving around. They are so well hidden deep down in the ocean that very few people know their whereabouts. And they can stay down for so long that in 1960, one sub, the USS *Triton*, completed the first submerged voyage right around the world. *Triton* took only 60 days and 21 hours to achieve the circumnavigation.

Hover time

Between 1968 and 2000, the SR.N4s, then the world's biggest hovercraft, whisked thousands of people across the English Channel from Dover to Calais every day. The largest of them could carry over 400 passengers and 60 cars at speeds of up to 80 mph (128 km/h). The 26-mile (42-km) crossing took barely half an hour— and once took just 22 minutes.

The factory machine

The biggest machines in the world are actually factories. Some factories need quite a lot of help from workers to make things. But in many of the largest car factories, more and more of the work is done by robots. Modern car factories, such as BMW's in Munich, are like scenes from *Transformers* with robot arms whirling relentlessly as they put together car after car.

CARS | The Essential Parts

The very first cars from 130 years ago were really horse carriages with an engine instead of a horse! Today's sleek, high-tech cars look very different. There are speciality models for racing and ones powered by clean energy. Some people also prefer the buzz of driving on just two wheels. Yet most vehicles have the same basic elements. Here's a quick guide before we begin.

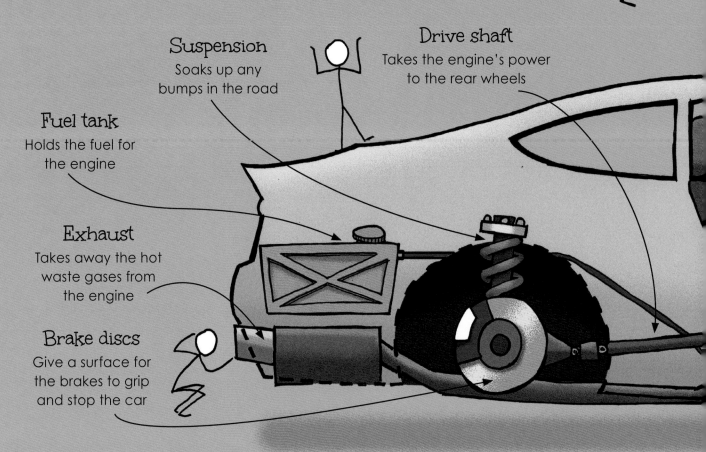

Suspension
Soaks up any bumps in the road

Drive shaft
Takes the engine's power to the rear wheels

Fuel tank
Holds the fuel for the engine

Exhaust
Takes away the hot waste gases from the engine

Brake discs
Give a surface for the brakes to grip and stop the car

Getting Gases Out

The exhaust pipes take away the waste gases left after the engine burns fuel. On their way, the gases pass through a box called a muffler, which muffles noise, and a catalytic converter, which makes the gases less poisonous.

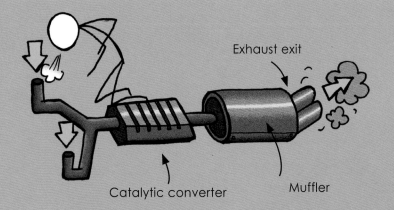

Exhaust exit

Catalytic converter

Muffler

Getting Fuel In

Fuel gets into the engine through a fuel injector. This is a valve that opens and shuts to spray the fuel into the engine's intake in regular spurts. Each spurt is precisely controlled by the car's electronic control system.

Fuel supply

Electromagnetic coil to pull the valve open

Magnet on the valve pulled by the coil

Spring to shut the valve

Fuel sprayed into the engine intake

Battery
Provides a store of electricity for when the engine's not running

Engine
Creates the power to move the car

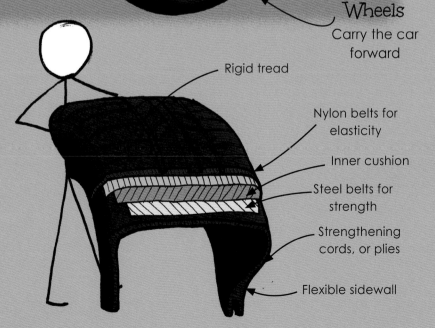

Wheels
Carry the car forward

Rigid tread

Nylon belts for elasticity

Inner cushion

Steel belts for strength

Strengthening cords, or plies

Flexible sidewall

Keeping You on the Road

Hard wheels would not only give a jolting ride, they would also slip all over the road and make the car difficult to control. So car wheels have rubber tires filled with a cushion of air to soak up bumps. The tread—the part of the tire in contact with the road—has an indented pattern to ensure a good grip.

CARS | Engine Power

Hundreds of times every second, tiny sparks set alight a mix of fuel and air inside the engine's cylinders on top of the piston. Just one-thousandth of a teaspoon of fuel burns each time. But it makes the air in the cylinder swell so violently that it punches the piston down, giving the engine its power.

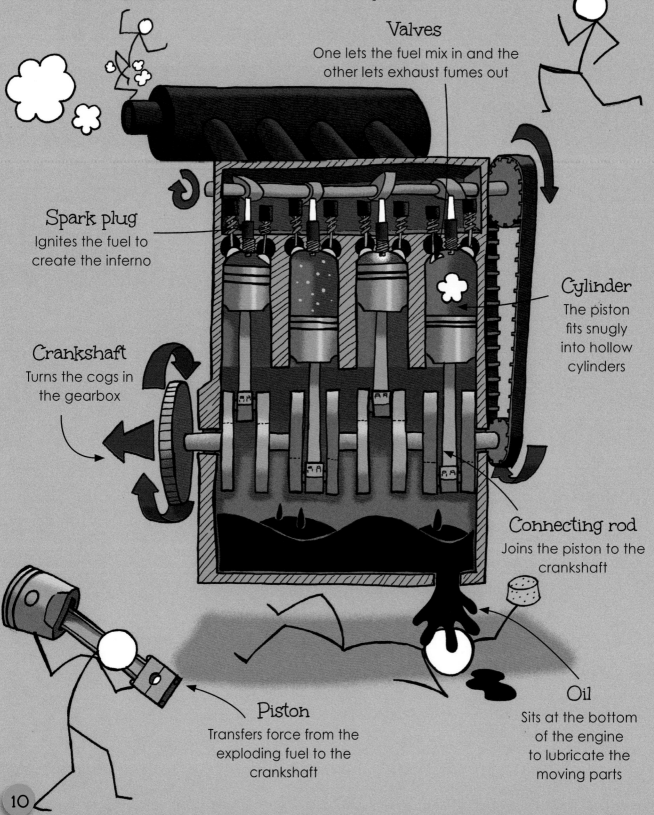

Valves
One lets the fuel mix in and the other lets exhaust fumes out

Spark plug
Ignites the fuel to create the inferno

Cylinder
The piston fits snugly into hollow cylinders

Crankshaft
Turns the cogs in the gearbox

Connecting rod
Joins the piston to the crankshaft

Piston
Transfers force from the exploding fuel to the crankshaft

Oil
Sits at the bottom of the engine to lubricate the moving parts

The Four-Stroke cycle

Each piston makes four strokes (up or down movements) for every bang. The whole cycle for just one piston is shown below.

1 **Suck (down stroke):** The piston moves down, sucking in air and a tiny squirt of gasoline through the inlet valve.

2 **Squeeze (up stroke):** The inlet valve at the top closes. The piston moves up, squeezing the air and gasoline together.

3 **Bang (down stroke):** When the piston reaches the top, a spark sets fire to the gasoline. The gas explodes, forcing the piston back down.

4 **Blow (up stroke):** The piston moves back up and pushes the burnt gases out of the outlet valve.

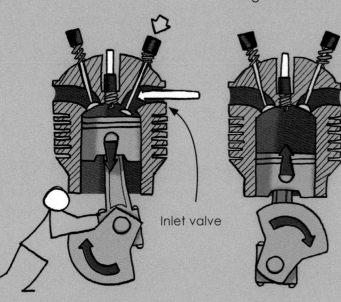
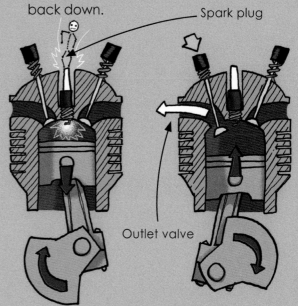

Spark plug

Inlet valve

Outlet valve

Getting in Gear

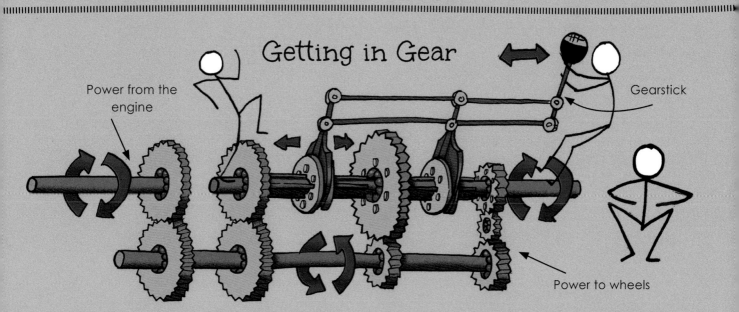

Power from the engine

Gearstick

Power to wheels

A car's gearbox contains pairs of cogs of varying sizes. One row sits on a shaft driven by the engine, and the other row sits on a shaft that drives the wheels. By using the gearstick, you can choose which pair does the job.

CARS | Wheels and Brakes

There's a lot more to a car's wheel than just a wheel!
Suspension deals with bumps to keep the wheel on the
road. The brakes act on the wheels to slow the car down or
stop it altogether. The steering swivels the front wheels to
take the car in a new direction.

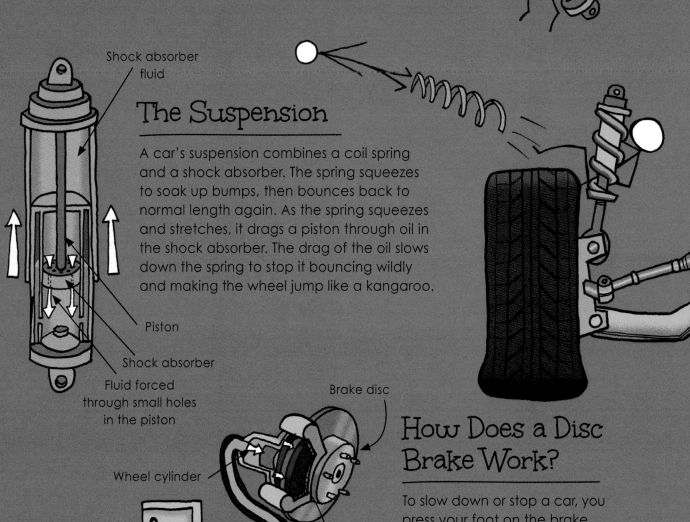

Shock absorber fluid

Piston

Shock absorber

Fluid forced through small holes in the piston

The Suspension

A car's suspension combines a coil spring
and a shock absorber. The spring squeezes
to soak up bumps, then bounces back to
normal length again. As the spring squeezes
and stretches, it drags a piston through oil in
the shock absorber. The drag of the oil slows
down the spring to stop it bouncing wildly
and making the wheel jump like a kangaroo.

Brake disc

Wheel cylinder

Brake pad

Brake pipes

Brake master cylinder

Brake pedal

How Does a Disc Brake Work?

To slow down or stop a car, you
press your foot on the brake
pedal. This moves a piston in the
brake master cylinder that forces
fluid through pipes to move pistons
in cylinders on each wheel.
These small pistons then squeeze
tough pads hard against brake
discs on each wheel, so that the
friction slows the wheel.

Rear-Wheel drive

In many cars in the past, the engine's power went to the rear wheels only, via a long drive shaft under the car. This is called rear-wheel drive. In most cars now, the drive goes to the front wheels instead. And in a few cars, especially those for driving off-road, power goes to all the wheels—four-wheel drive.

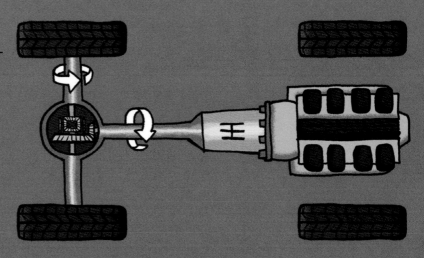

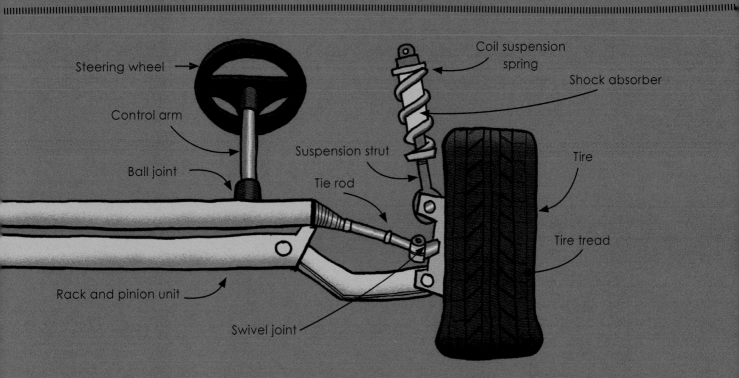

Steering wheel

Control arm

Ball joint

Suspension strut

Tie rod

Coil suspension spring

Shock absorber

Tire

Tire tread

Rack and pinion unit

Swivel joint

How Does the Steering Work?

To steer a car, you turn the steering wheel. This swivels the front wheels via the steering shaft, which ends in a pinion. Teeth on the pinion interlock with teeth on a bar called the rack. As the pinion turns, it moves the rack left or right. In most cars now, the steering is power-assisted by hydraulics or an electric motor.

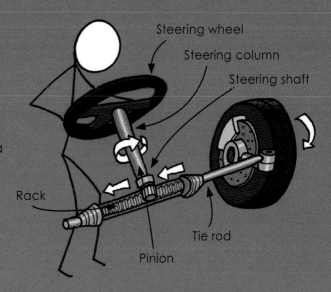

Steering wheel

Steering column

Steering shaft

Rack

Pinion

Tie rod

CARS | Advanced Systems

There is much more to a modern car than just power, steering, and brakes. Cars have a range of systems to help keep you safe in a crash, find your route, park neatly for you, and even do all the driving! More and more of the driver's tasks are being taken over by electronic systems. In the future, people may just speak to their phone to get their car to drive up and take them to their destination!

Airbags can also make great bouncy cushions

Crash Safety

Every year 1.2 million people are killed in road accidents around the world and 50 million are injured. That's why cars have safety systems to protect passengers. Seat belts stop passengers being hurled forward druing a crash. Airbags inflate instantly to stop passengers being flung against the steering wheel or dashboard.

Crumple Zone

The area where the passengers sit is protected with a strong cage. But the car outside the cage is a crumple zone. This means it is designed to crumple up in a controlled way and absorb some of the shock in a crash. Each car design is crash-tested to make sure the crumple zone and cage keep passengers safe.

Where in the World?

In the old days, people used maps to find their way. Now, most cars are equipped with Global Positioning System (GPS). GPS uses timed radio signals from satellites in space to tell your system exactly where you are. It works by calculating how long the signals take to reach it from three or four satellites. That tells it exactly how far away each satellite is. By comparing the distances, it can work out exactly where you are.

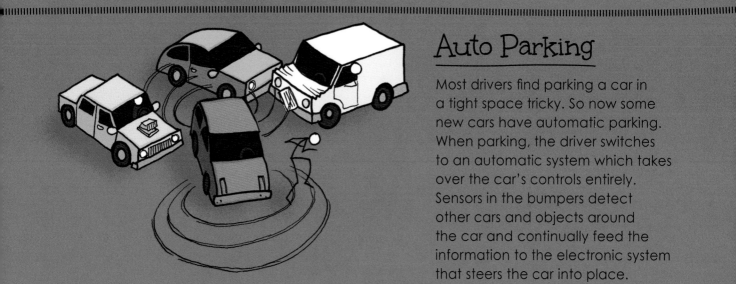

Auto Parking

Most drivers find parking a car in a tight space tricky. So now some new cars have automatic parking. When parking, the driver switches to an automatic system which takes over the car's controls entirely. Sensors in the bumpers detect other cars and objects around the car and continually feed the information to the electronic system that steers the car into place.

Driverless Cars

Soon you may get in a car that can drive itself! Driverless cars are like robots. They are controlled by computer, using laser systems to detect objects in their way. They are still experimental, and in the US can only be tested on public roads in California, Michigan, Florida, and Nevada. Google is testing a driverless car that looks like any other car from the outside, but it has neither a steering wheel nor other driver controls.

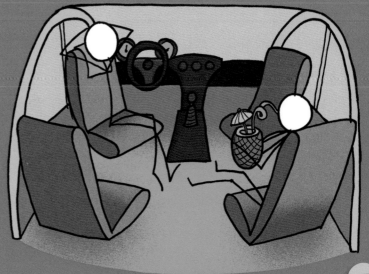

SPECIALITY CARS | Formula One Cars

Formula One (F1) cars have ultralight bodies and incredibly powerful engines so that they can hurtle round the race track at speeds of more than 200 miles per hour. To keep them stable, they are built very low. But there's not much room for the driver, who has to squeeze in and lie back less than an inch from the ground!

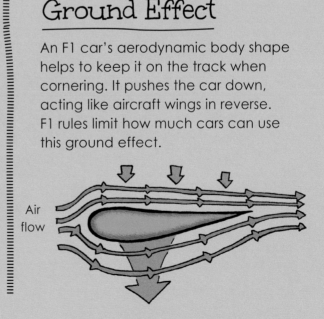

Ground Effect

An F1 car's aerodynamic body shape helps to keep it on the track when cornering. It pushes the car down, acting like aircraft wings in reverse. F1 rules limit how much cars can use this ground effect.

Air flow

Light Body

F1 racing cars are said to be *monocoque*. That's French for "single shell." It means the body is made out of one piece of material. That material is usually a special strong but light substance, such as carbon fiber.

Driver Controls

In a racing car, almost all the controls are on the steering wheel! The driver changes gear with one finger, and there are lots of controls to tune the engine on the move. There's also a screen displaying track conditions and instructions from the race team and track officials.

1. Pit lane speed limiter
2. Differential +
3. Engine push
4. Gear upshift
5. Traction control +
6. Engine push setting switch
7. Clutch lever
8. Traction control
9. Team info in-lap
10. Burn out
11. Multifunctional switch
12. Lambda (fuel-air mix)
13. Diagnostic
14. Wing angle info switch
15. Clutch
16. Differential selective switch
17. Team radio
18. Traction control -
19. Gear downshift
20. Engine break
21. Differential -
22. Neutral
23. Display page change

Slick tires

F1 cars have extremely wide slick tires for maximum grip on the track. They are called slicks because they don't have an indented tread pattern like normal road tires. That means they can't cut through water, but they ensure a large area of rubber makes contact with the track.

SPECIALITY CARS | Hybrid, Electric, and Solar-Powered

When gasoline and diesel (combustion) engines burn fuel, they chuck out a lot of gases via the exhaust that pollute the air. Pollution from car exhausts not only damages people's health, it also damages the world's climate. So many car manufacturers are now looking for cleaner ways to power cars.

Gasoline and Electric

One well-tested idea is the hybrid car. This has both a gasoline engine and an electric motor sharing the task of powering the car. In some hybrids, there is just a small gasoline engine running at a steady speed for cruising, while the electric motor does most of the work. In others, the gasoline engine does more of the work.

1. When the car is accelerating, batteries supply power to the electric motor.

2. When the car is cruising, the engine tops up the power of the motor.

3. When the car is slowing down, the motor becomes an electric generator, charging the batteries.

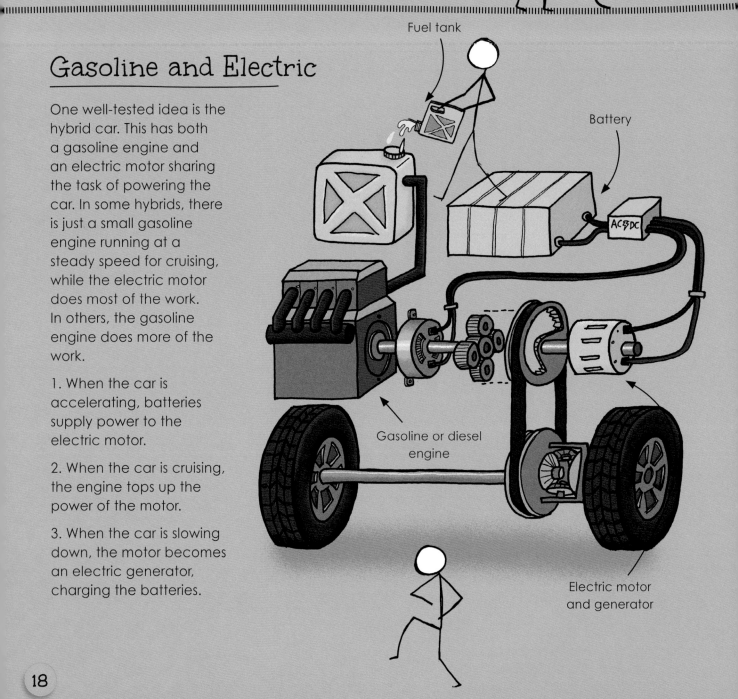

Fuel tank

Battery

Gasoline or diesel engine

Electric motor and generator

Electric Only

Electric cars are very clean because they are powered entirely by an electric motor and burn no fuel. But the car must be plugged into an electrical socket to recharge the batteries after each journey. Charging points can be hard to find even in big cities.

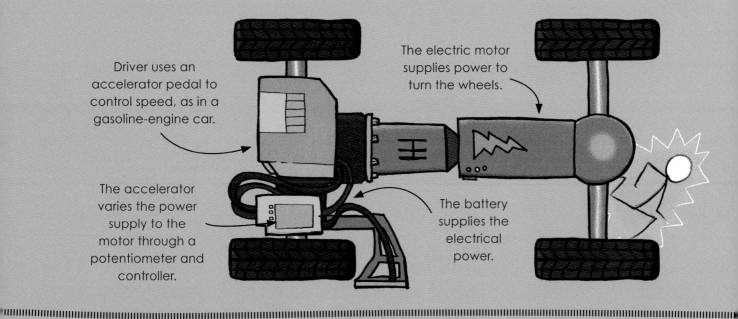

Driver uses an accelerator pedal to control speed, as in a gasoline-engine car.

The electric motor supplies power to turn the wheels.

The accelerator varies the power supply to the motor through a potentiometer and controller.

The battery supplies the electrical power.

Power from the Sun

Wouldn't it be great if cars could be powered entirely by the sun? That's the idea behind solar cars, which have solar cells on the roof to convert sunlight into electricity. The problem is that solar cells don't provide enough power, and it isn't always sunny. So solar cars aren't very practical yet.

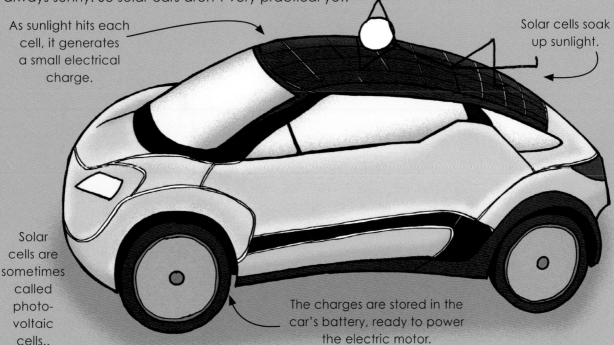

As sunlight hits each cell, it generates a small electrical charge.

Solar cells soak up sunlight.

Solar cells are sometimes called photovoltaic cells..

The charges are stored in the car's battery, ready to power the electric motor.

Motorcycles

Some people like riding motorcycles for the thrill of it. Others think bikes are a good way to get around in overcrowded cities. But all motorcycles work in much the same way. In between the two wheels is an engine that drives the back wheel via a chain or a shaft. The rider steers by turning the front wheel with the handlebars and by leaning the bike over.

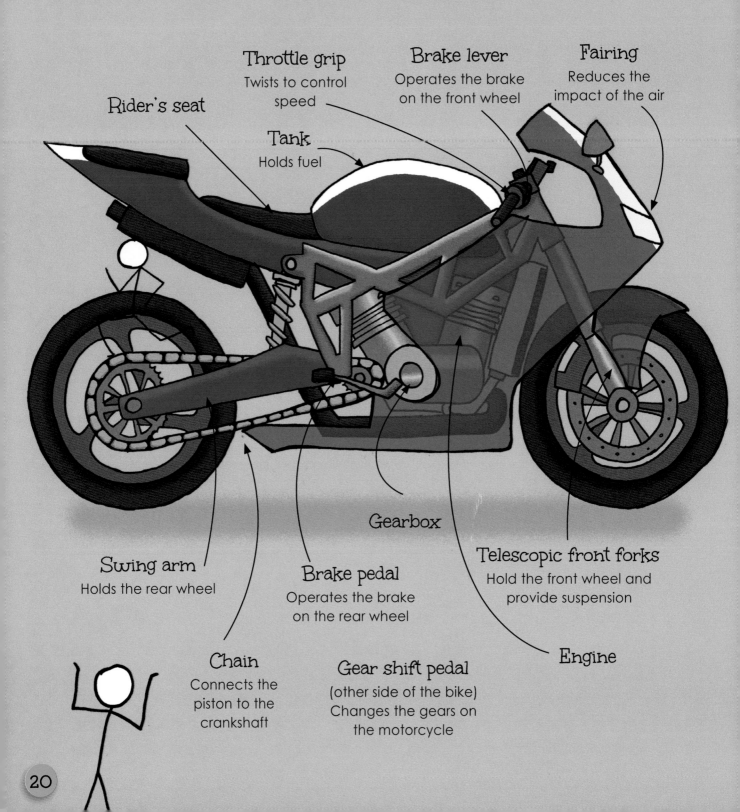

Throttle grip
Twists to control speed

Brake lever
Operates the brake on the front wheel

Fairing
Reduces the impact of the air

Rider's seat

Tank
Holds fuel

Gearbox

Swing arm
Holds the rear wheel

Brake pedal
Operates the brake on the rear wheel

Telescopic front forks
Hold the front wheel and provide suspension

Engine

Chain
Connects the piston to the crankshaft

Gear shift pedal
(other side of the bike)
Changes the gears on the motorcycle

Front Forks

The front wheel of a motorcycle is held between the two prongs of the front forks. The forks turn with the handlebars, allowing the rider to swivel the front wheel. They are called telescopic forks. This is because when the bike goes over a bump, the bottom half of each prong slides up into the top half, like a collapsing telescope. Inside the top is a spring and shock absorber to provide the bike's suspension.

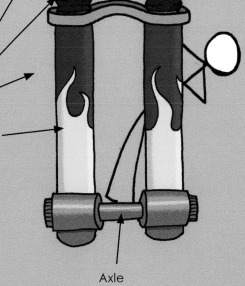

Fixed fork

Triple tree

Rubber gaiter

Active fork

Hydraulic chamber

Axle

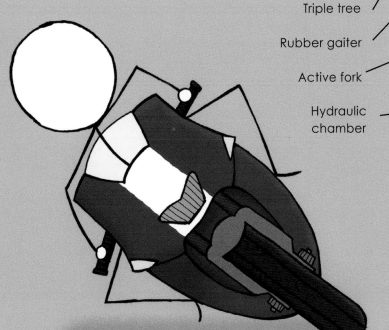

Leaning into Bends

Even though they have just two wheels, bikes stay upright easily on the move because, like spinning tops, the wheels are naturally stable. This effect is described as gyroscopic. But when going around bends in the road, the rider must lean the bike over. This is to counteract the centrifugal force that flings the bike outwards. The bike leans at an angle where the force of gravity that would make it fall over exactly balances the centrifugal force.

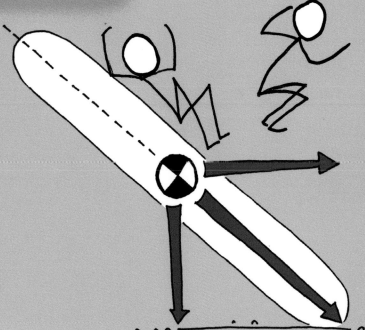

TRAINS | The Essential Parts

Unlike cars, which can be steered in any direction you choose, trains are kept firmly in the direction of the railroad tracks by the lips, or flanges, on their wheels. This means a long chain of carriages or trucks can be linked together behind a single engine or locomotive. High-speed trains and many other electric trains pick up their electricity as they go along from overhead cables or extra live rails. But sometimes it isn't practical to install an electricity supply. So diesel electric locomotives carry their supply with them.

Alternator
Uses the rotation provided by the diesel to generate electricity. An alternator generates an alternating current (AC) that continually switches direction

Air intake
Draws in air to mix the diesel fuel to power the diesel engine

Turbocharger
Boosts the flow of fuel and air into the engine

Main diesel engine
Provides power for the generator and compressor

Compressor
The engine powers an air compressor at the rear of the locomotive as well as generating electricity

Exhaust
Takes out waste gases from the diesel engine

The fuel tank
Carries fuel for the engine (on other side of the air tanks)

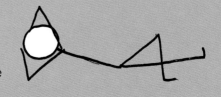

The Cab

The driver sits in a cab at the front or the rear of the locomotive. Being at the rear gives a less clear view ahead but makes it easier for the driver and guard to communicate. In the cab there are gauges for oil pressure and fuel, engine speed and generator output, and a speedometer. There are also buttons to start or stop the engine and levers to apply the air brakes, control the power, change direction, and spray out sand.

Rectifier

Switches the alternating current (AC) to direct current (DC) for the motors

Modern Diesel Electric

In the US, most railroads mostly use locomotives with diesel engines that don't drive the wheels directly. Instead, these engines drive generators that makes electricity to power the electric motors that drive the wheels. The latest locomotives can travel at 125 mph.

Sand

Helps to stop the wheels slipping. It is sprayed by compressed air onto the track in front of the wheels

Electric traction motors

Drive the wheels. They are set down between the wheels and connected to the engine only by an electric cable

Air tanks

The compressed air is stored in tanks under the locomotive, ready to be released to push on the brakes

Regenerative braking

Turns the electric motors into electricity generators, both to slow down the loco and generate bonus electricity

TRAINS | Electric Trains

Imagine darting across the landscape twice as fast as a Formula One racing car—while eating your dinner. Well, you can do just that if you step aboard a high-speed electric train. There are none this fast in the US yet, but there are electric trains that travel over 280 miles per hour in western Europe, China, and Japan. And because they pick up their power from electric cables, they are clean as well as fast.

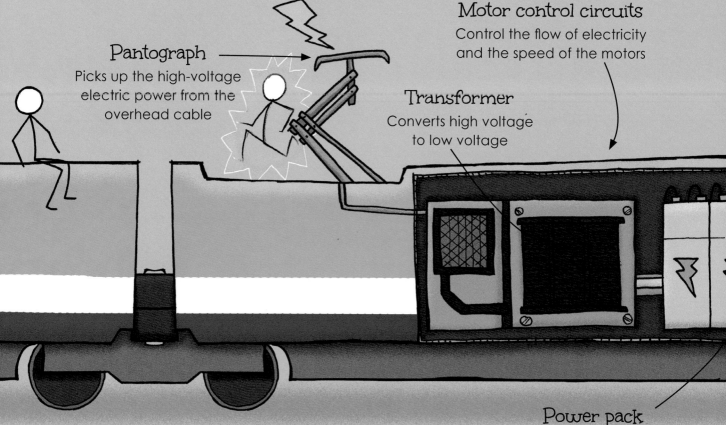

Motor control circuits
Control the flow of electricity and the speed of the motors

Pantograph
Picks up the high-voltage electric power from the overhead cable

Transformer
Converts high voltage to low voltage

Power pack

Power

As they whiz along, high-speed trains pick up high-voltage electricity from an overhead cable through a long arm called a pantograph. Inside the locomotive, a transformer converts the high voltage into the low voltage needed by the motors. The flow of electricity to the motors, and thus the speed of the train, is controlled by electronic circuits.

Inside the Cab

In the cab of a German ICE (Inter-City Express) high-speed train, all the controls are at the driver's fingertips. A dial on the left shows engine power, the other one, train speed. Display screens provide data on the train's systems and performance. A continuous train control (LZB) system comes into operation when the train is traveling fast. This continually feeds signals to the driver showing if the track ahead is clear and applies the brakes if the driver doesn't react.

Freon tanks
Filled with liquid Freon gas, tanks surround the electronics and keep them cool

Cab

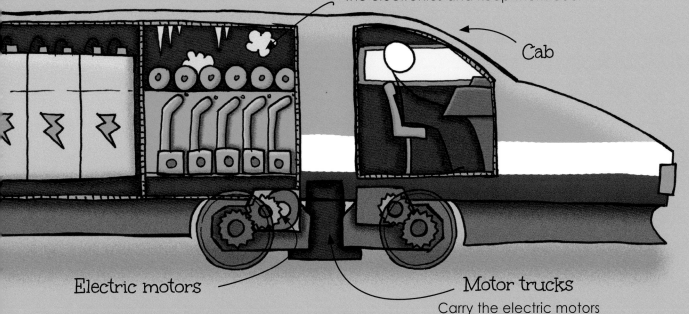

Electric motors

Motor trucks
Carry the electric motors that drive the wheels

Staying on Track

Trains are kept on track by the shape of their wheels. Each wheel has a lip, or flange, that sits inside each rail and stops the train moving sideways. Tracks for ordinary trains are laid on a bed of loose stones, or ballast, to keep costs down. But high-speed trains run on a ballastless track: a bed of solid concrete that ensures smooth running.

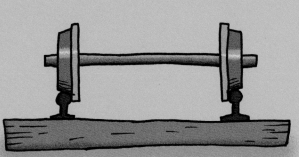

TRAINS | High-Speed Maglevs

The fastest trains in the world have no wheels and no engine. Instead they float above the track and whiz along entirely due to the power of electromagnetism. They are called maglevs (short for "magnetic levitation"). At the moment, most run only short distances, or are experimental. But in spring 2015, a full-sized maglev test train in Japan whooshed along at 374 miles per hour—faster than any train has traveled before!

When opposite poles of magnets meet, they pull each other together.

When matching poles of magnets meet, they push each other apart.

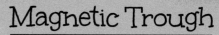

Magnetic Trough

In one maglev system, there are powerful magnets in both the train and the track, and the train floats inside a magnetic trough. This is called electrodynamic suspension, or EDS. The magnets in the train are extremely strong 'superconducting' magnets. They gain power by chilling the coils dramatically in liquid nitrogen to below -300°F (-184°C).

Pole to Pole

A magnet has two different ends, or poles. When two magnets meet, the like poles push apart and opposite poles pull together. An EDS track always has a north pole magnet on one side and a south pole magnet on the other. By alternately pushing and pulling the magnets in the train, they pass it along in a relay and make it float.

Matching poles in the train and track continually meet to keep the train floating between and above the track.

The alternation of polarity in the track magnets drives the train forward by a mix of magnetic repulsion and attraction.

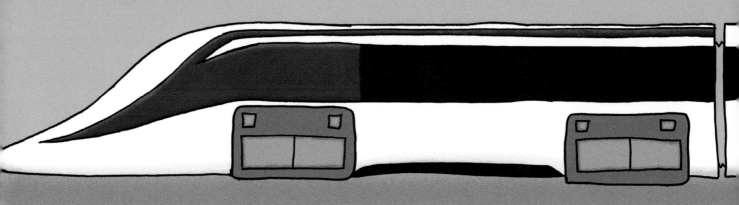

Ghostly Glider

Japan's experimental EDS maglev has just one train and one track so far. Yet it can already travel at 374 mph. To run it, a special magnetic track is to be built all the way from Tokyo to Osaka. It won't be open until the year 2045, but the train will glide along like a ghost as it covers the 250-mile journey silently and cleanly in barely an hour.

Hanging Trains

In another maglev system, the track is just steel and all the magnets are in the train. The train's magnets wrap around the track in a C-shape.

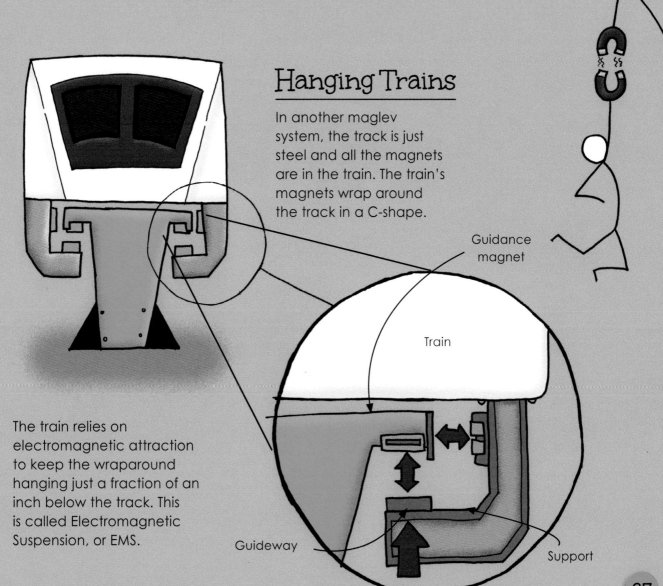

Guidance magnet

Train

The train relies on electromagnetic attraction to keep the wraparound hanging just a fraction of an inch below the track. This is called Electromagnetic Suspension, or EMS.

Guideway

Support

Modern Airliners

Airliners—planes that carry passengers—are complicated machines. Yet, like most aircraft, they have just three main parts: fuselage, wings, and engines. The fuselage is the long tube where the pilot, passengers, and luggage are carried. Two big wings on either side lift the aircraft, and two little wings and a fin at the rear provide control. The engines power the aircraft through the air.

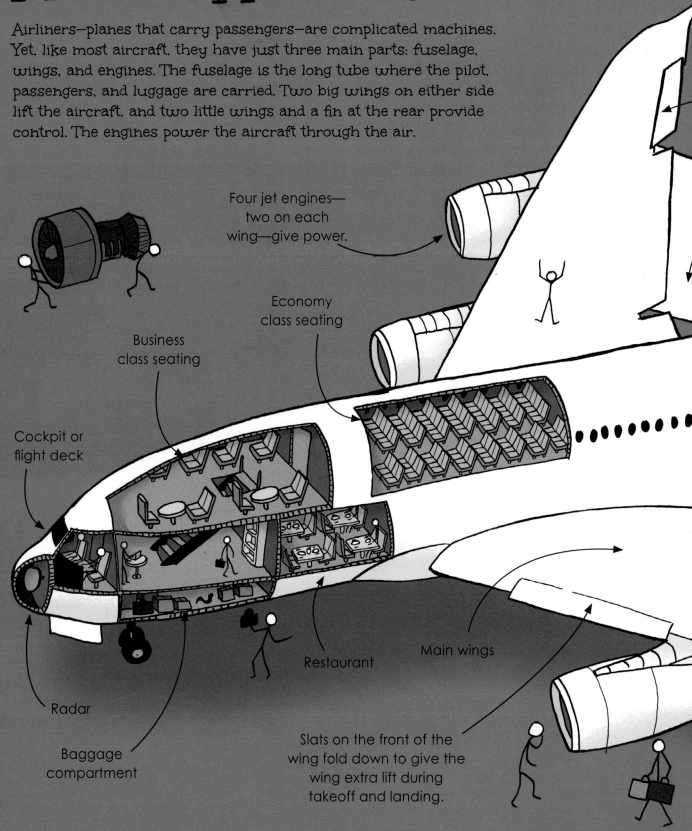

Four jet engines— two on each wing—give power.

Economy class seating

Business class seating

Cockpit or flight deck

Restaurant

Main wings

Radar

Baggage compartment

Slats on the front of the wing fold down to give the wing extra lift during takeoff and landing.

Inside an Airliner

This is the world's largest airliner, the Airbus A380. It has two decks and can carry up to 853 people at a time. It's so big that some versions have bars and restaurants for passengers to use on long flights.

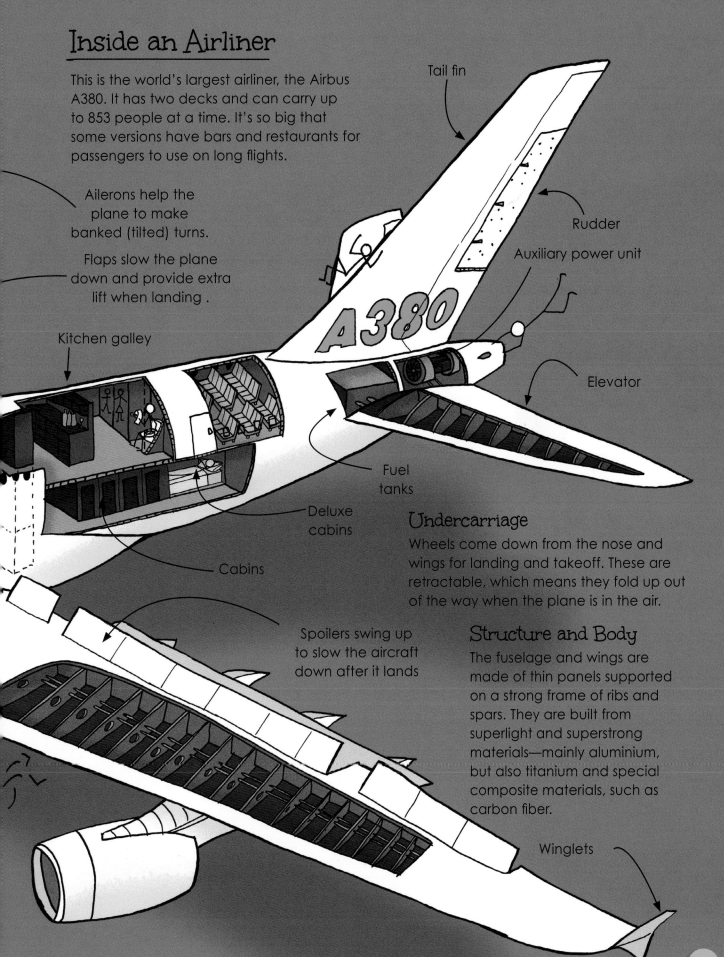

Tail fin

Rudder

Auxiliary power unit

Ailerons help the plane to make banked (tilted) turns.

Flaps slow the plane down and provide extra lift when landing .

Kitchen galley

Elevator

Fuel tanks

Deluxe cabins

Cabins

Spoilers swing up to slow the aircraft down after it lands

Undercarriage
Wheels come down from the nose and wings for landing and takeoff. These are retractable, which means they fold up out of the way when the plane is in the air.

Structure and Body
The fuselage and wings are made of thin panels supported on a strong frame of ribs and spars. They are built from superlight and superstrong materials—mainly aluminium, but also titanium and special composite materials, such as carbon fiber.

Winglets

Wings

While a plane is moving fast enough, its wings provide the lift that keeps it airborne. As wings slice through the air (top right), air is forced up and over them. The air stretches out and drops in pressure so the wings are pushed up by the higher air pressure beneath. The pilot controls the plane by moving flaps on the wing edges to vary the lift that each wing provides.

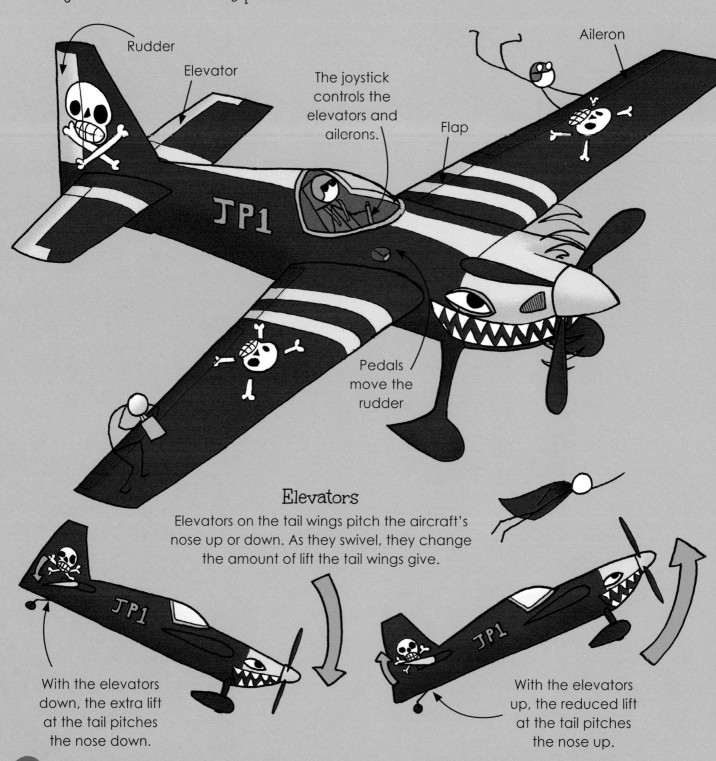

Rudder

Elevator

The joystick controls the elevators and ailerons.

Aileron

Flap

JP1

Pedals move the rudder

Elevators

Elevators on the tail wings pitch the aircraft's nose up or down. As they swivel, they change the amount of lift the tail wings give.

With the elevators down, the extra lift at the tail pitches the nose down.

With the elevators up, the reduced lift at the tail pitches the nose up.

The Shape of Wings

Wings work because they have a special curved shape, or camber, and cut through the air at a slight angle called the angle of attack. This is what forces the air up and over to create lift. Up to a point, the greater the camber and angle of attack, the greater the lift.

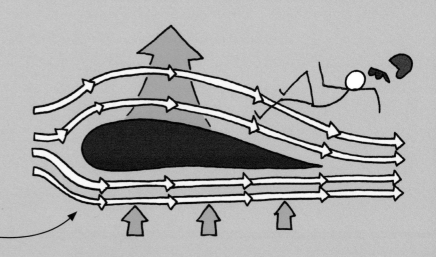

Ailerons

Ailerons make the plane roll to left or right by lifting one wing more than the other. In combination with the rudder, they enable the plane to bank and turn.

Left aileron up, right aileron down makes the plane roll to the left.

Left aileron down, right aileron up makes the plane roll to the right.

Rudder

The rudder is the upright flap on the tail. Swinging it to the left makes the plane steer, or yaw, left. Swinging it to the right makes it steer right.

Flaps

Lowering the flaps helps the plane to land. It slows the plane down by increasing drag and generates the extra lift needed to keep the plane in the air at slow speeds.

Flight Controls

There is no road to guide you up in the air, so pilots rely on instruments to tell them where they are and which way to go. In modern airliners, the instruments are linked to the plane's control systems and fly the plane automatically most of the time.

Six Pack

All planes still have six basic instruments. These are now mostly backups in case the electronic display fails.

1 The airspeed indicator shows how fast the plane is flying in knots. A knot is just a little more than 1 mph.

2 The attitude indicator or artificial horizon shows how level the plane is flying—for example, if it is banked to one side or pitched to nose or tail.

3 The altimeter shows how far above the ground the plane is flying in feet.

4 The turn indicator shows how fast and steeply the plane is banking on a turn.

5 The heading indicator is a compass. It shows the pilot which direction the plane is heading and allows the plane to fly on a chosen compass bearing.

6. The vertical speed indicator shows how fast the plane is climbing or descending.

Fly-by-Wire

In old planes, the pilot's controls moved the wing flaps through rods and levers. Modern planes are fly-by-wire: electric wires simply control motors that move the flaps.

In manual flight, the pilot's controls operate a computer that sends signals through wires to move the flaps.

In autopilot, the plane's flight control computer takes over from the pilot, making adjustments to the flight automatically in response to data from the instruments.

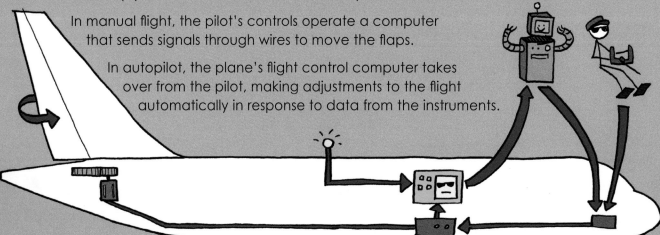

Captain's Seat

The flight captain sits in the left-hand seat and the copilot in the right-hand seat of the cockpit. The copilot has exactly the same controls as the captain.

Primary flight display
All the basic instruments, including the artificial horizon and airspeed indicator, are combined in a single electronic screen display.

Autopilot
The pilot usually controls the plane manually for takeoff and landing, and switches on the autopilot once the plane is at cruising height.

Sidestick
In manual flight, the pilot controls the flaps using the handle at their side, called a sidestick.

Navigation display
The navigation display feeds information from satellites, radio beacons, and radar to an electronic map showing everything the pilot needs to know.

Engine display
This gives a continual update on how the engines are performing.

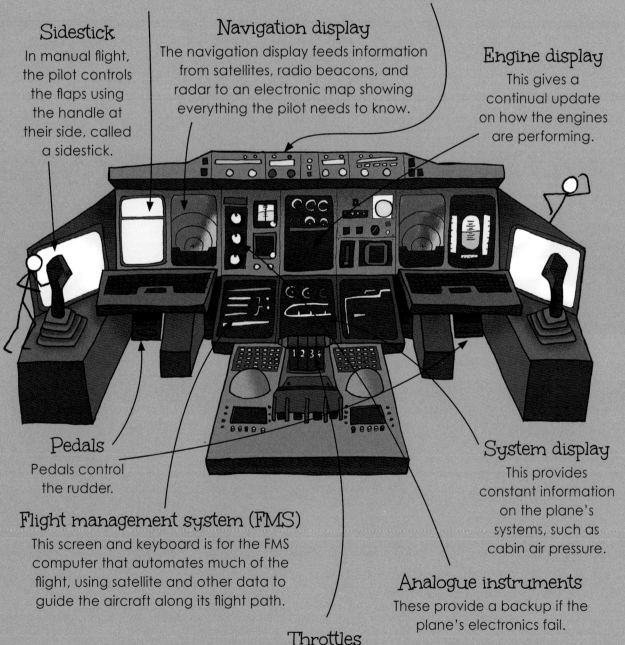

Pedals
Pedals control the rudder.

Flight management system (FMS)
This screen and keyboard is for the FMS computer that automates much of the flight, using satellite and other data to guide the aircraft along its flight path.

System display
This provides constant information on the plane's systems, such as cabin air pressure.

Analogue instruments
These provide a backup if the plane's electronics fail.

Throttles
There is a throttle control for each of the four engines. Pushing the lever forward increases the power.

Jet Engines

Like cars, planes used to have engines with heavy pistons that clanked up and down. Most bigger planes now have jet engines. These engines have only fans that whiz around inside a tube, gulping in huge quantities of air. They are very powerful and light, but they are noisy and only work well at high speeds.

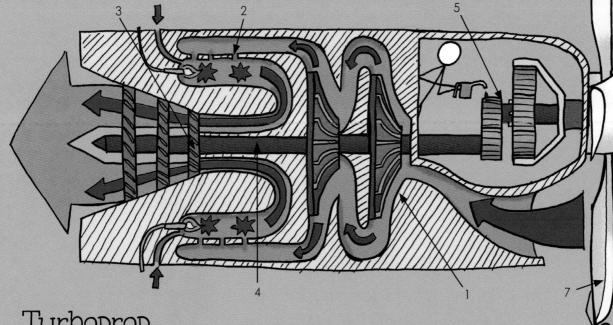

Turboprop

Many smaller airplanes and cargo planes have turboprop engines. These are jet engines that turn a propeller and work well at lower speeds than a turbofan jet engine.

1   Air is drawn in the front of the engine by a fan.

2   The air is mixed with fuel and ignited in the combustion chamber.

3   The burning fuel and air expand and push against a kind of fan called a turbine, spinning it around.

4   As the turbine spins, it turns the drive shaft and a gear box.

5   The gear box sets the propeller spinning.

6   The spinning propeller.

7   The propeller pulls the plane along.

Cutting Edge

The propeller blades on turboprops are usually curved back like a scimitar sword. Like swept-back wings, the curve stops them dragging so much as they cut very fast through the air.

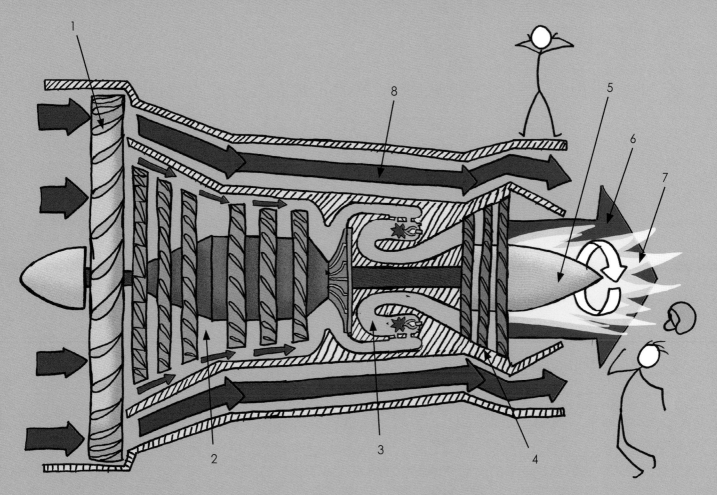

Turbofan

Most modern airliners use a variation on the basic jet engine called a turbofan. This has a second large fan at the front to draw in an extra flow of air that bypasses the engine core where the fuel and air burn. This makes the engine run more quietly at takeoff speeds.

1   A large fan sucks in air at the front.

2   Some of the air is blown into the compressor fan.

3   The compressor fan squeezes the air into the combustion chamber where it is mixed with jet fuel and set alight.

4   The burning fuel expands rapidly and rushes past each turbine's blades, spinning them like a windmill.

5   The spinning turbine spins the compressor fan.

6   The hot gases roar out very fast from the back of the engine as a hot jet.

7   As the jet shoots backwards out of the engine, it thrusts the plane forward.

8   The bypass air is blown around the outside of the combustion chamber and straight out the back.

Massive Fan

Turbofans are easily identified by the giant fan in the front of the engine.

Alternative Power

Jets are very noisy and the fuel they burn is expensive and causes pollution. So aircraft designers are experimenting with electric, solar, and even pedal power as alternative ways of powering planes. These experiments include the Solar Impulse project, with its two operational solar-powered aircraft.

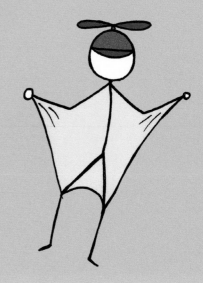

Sun Power

Solar planes have huge panels of solar cells on the wings. These convert sunlight into electricity to power electric motors. On the solar plane Solar Impulse 2, the solar panels also charge up a bank of lithium batteries during the day so the plane can fly at night.

Solar Impulse 2

Solar Impulse 2 is the most ambitious solar-powered plane yet. It can fly long distances by combining chargeable batteries with solar power. In 2015, it began an attempt to fly around the world by flying five days and five nights nonstop across the Pacific Ocean.

Wings are covered in 17,000 solar cells

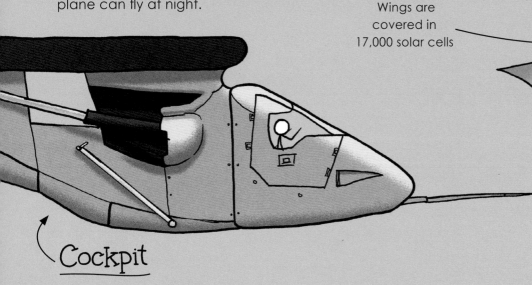

Cockpit

As Solar Impulse 2 flies around the world, the pilot will have to sit alone in the cockpit for five or six days at a time. The tiny cockpit has no air conditioning, so it can get very hot or very cold. There is a parachute and a life raft if things go wrong . . .

Plug-in Planes

Electric planes fly almost as silently as a glider, but for now they can only make short flights. In 2015, the Airbus E-fan was the first electric-powered plane to fly across the English Channel.

Pedal Power

Modern lightweight materials have made human-powered aircraft (HPAs) possible. In 1988 the experimental HPA, Daedalus 88, flew 71.5 miles (115 km) over the Mediterranean Sea from Crete to the Greek island of Santorini.

Daedalus was named after a mythical Greek inventor who made feather wings and managed to fly.

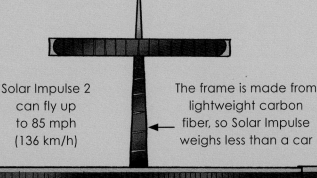

Solar Impulse 2 can fly up to 85 mph (136 km/h)

The frame is made from lightweight carbon fiber, so Solar Impulse weighs less than a car

Solar Impulse 2 wingspan is 236 ft (72 m)

Four electric motors turn the propellers

Each motor has the power of a small motorcycle

Giant Wings

Solar Impulse 2 needs a vast solar-panel area to catch enough sun to power it. It also needs a lot of lift because it flies very slowly. So its wingspan is over 230 ft (70 m)—wider than a jumbo jet's.

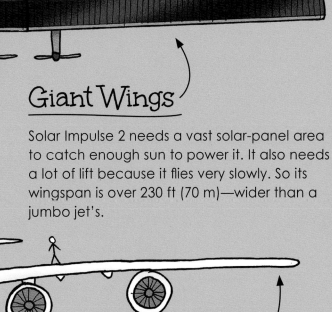

Boeing 747 wingspan is 225 ft (68.5 m)

Vertical Takeoff

Most ordinary planes need a long runway to build up the speed to lift off. Vertical takeoff and landing planes (VTOL) have the same fixed wings but also special engines that can power them straight up into the air for takeoff and lower them gently for landing.

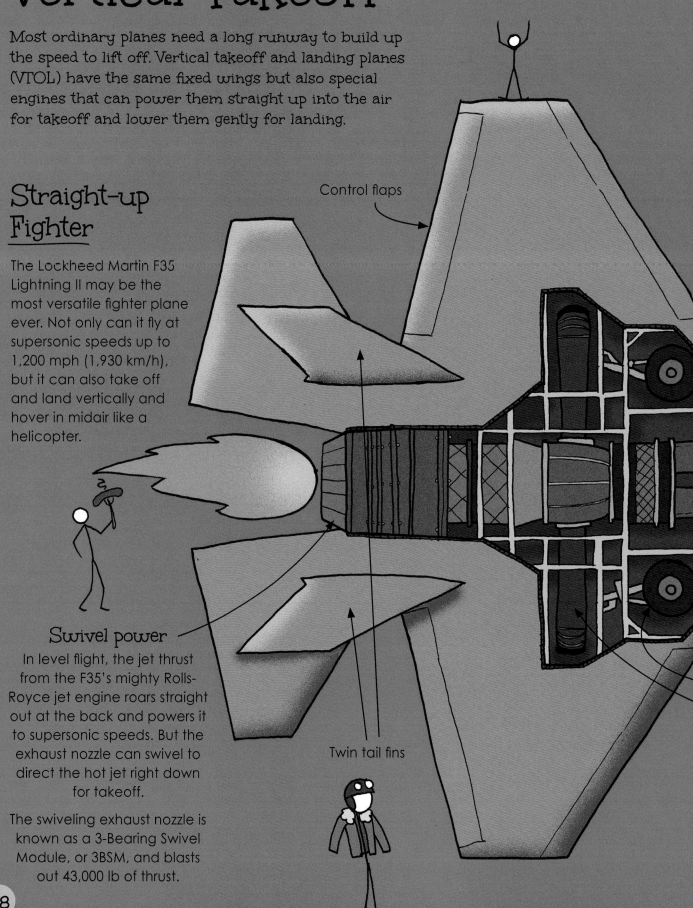

Straight-up Fighter

The Lockheed Martin F35 Lightning II may be the most versatile fighter plane ever. Not only can it fly at supersonic speeds up to 1,200 mph (1,930 km/h), but it can also take off and land vertically and hover in midair like a helicopter.

Control flaps

Twin tail fins

Swivel power

In level flight, the jet thrust from the F35's mighty Rolls-Royce jet engine roars straight out at the back and powers it to supersonic speeds. But the exhaust nozzle can swivel to direct the hot jet right down for takeoff.

The swiveling exhaust nozzle is known as a 3-Bearing Swivel Module, or 3BSM, and blasts out 43,000 lb of thrust.

Up and Down

To take off vertically, or in a short space, the F35 opens the lift fan doors and turns the swivel jet to point down. At once, a surge of cool air from the lift fan and hot air from the swivel jet thrusts the plane upwards. The plane rises powerfully into the air, kept in balance by the roll posts.

To hover, the F35 keeps the downthrust from the lift fan in balance with the weight of the plane.

To land, the F35 reverses the takeoff procedure, gradually reducing power to lower the plane.

Upper fan doors

Air intake

Radar

Cockpit

Missile bay

Landing gear in wheel bay, which can be used for both vertical and horizontal takeoff

Lift Fan

Just behind the cockpit is the lift fan. This super-powerful fan is mounted horizontally and driven by a shaft from the engine. There are two fans rotating in opposite directions and blowing out cool air.

Upthrust

In level flight, the lift fan is hidden under folding doors. But for vertical takeoff, the doors open. Air is then sucked in through the top of the fan and blasted out through the bottom to create an upthrust of over 40,000 lb that powers the plane straight up.

Roll posts

To steady the plane when taking off and hovering, the pilot can fire the jet thrusters in each wing. These get their power through ducts from the main engine, called roll posts. Each delivers about 1,000 lb of thrust.

Helicopters

Ordinary aircraft must fly forward nonstop for the wings to lift them. But a helicopter's wings are rotor blades that give lift simply by spinning around and around. That's why helicopters can take off and land almost vertically and hover in midair.

The Tail Rotor

One potential problem is that the helicopter itself, rather than the rotor blades, might spin around. This is solved by a small vertical tail rotor that pulls the helicopter around in the opposite direction to the rotors.

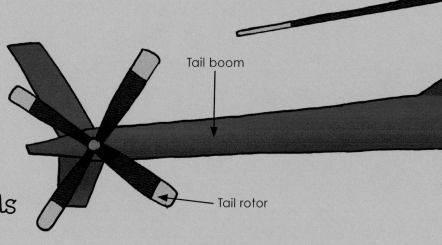

Tail boom

Tail rotor

Forward, Backwards and Sideways

Normally, the rotor pulls the helicopter straight up. But the pilot can tilt the blades to increase or reduce the pitch at a particular point as they go round. This is called cyclic pitch control and angles the blades ahead, behind, left, or right so the helicopter can fly in that direction.

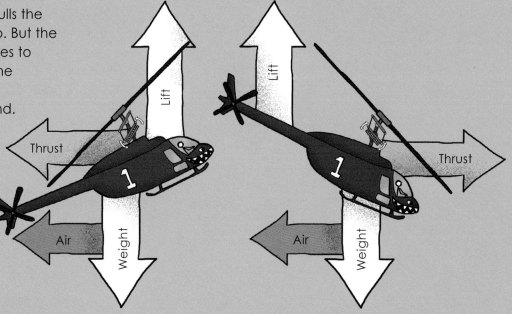

Lift

Thrust

Air

Weight

Lift

Thrust

Air

Weight

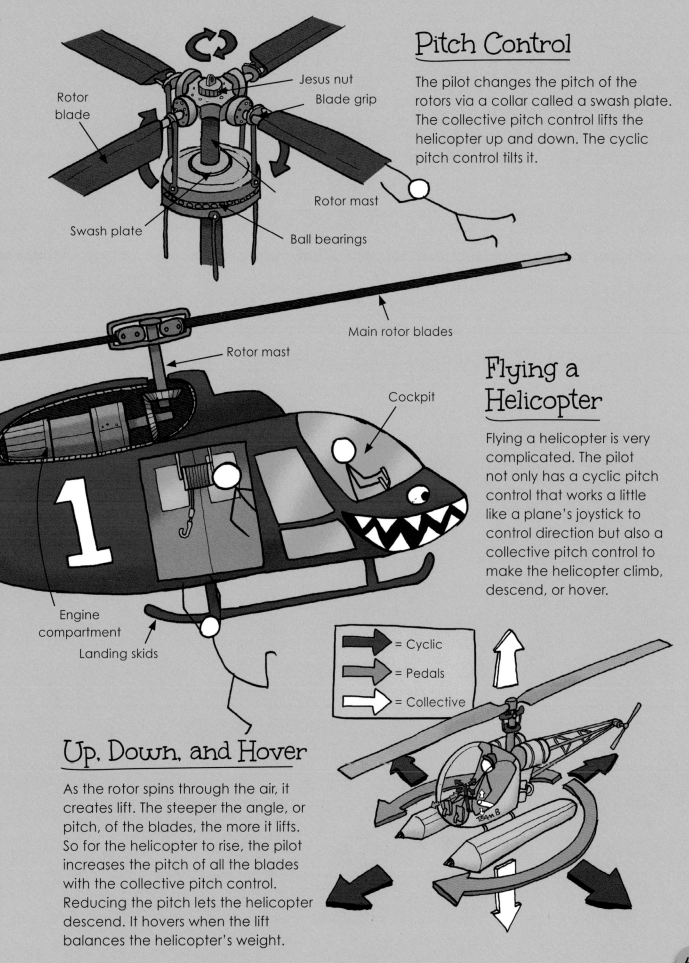

Pitch Control

The pilot changes the pitch of the rotors via a collar called a swash plate. The collective pitch control lifts the helicopter up and down. The cyclic pitch control tilts it.

Jesus nut

Blade grip

Rotor blade

Rotor mast

Swash plate

Ball bearings

Main rotor blades

Rotor mast

Cockpit

Flying a Helicopter

Flying a helicopter is very complicated. The pilot not only has a cyclic pitch control that works a little like a plane's joystick to control direction but also a collective pitch control to make the helicopter climb, descend, or hover.

Engine compartment

Landing skids

= Cyclic

= Pedals

= Collective

Up, Down, and Hover

As the rotor spins through the air, it creates lift. The steeper the angle, or pitch, of the blades, the more it lifts. So for the helicopter to rise, the pilot increases the pitch of all the blades with the collective pitch control. Reducing the pitch lets the helicopter descend. It hovers when the lift balances the helicopter's weight.

Balloons and Airships

You don't always need wings to fly. Balloons and airships float up into the air using gases lighter than air. Some balloons are bags filled with hot air or light helium gas to make them rise. Airships are lifted by a long, semi-rigid envelope filled with helium. You can't steer a hot-air balloon, which goes where the wind blows it. But you can fly in the direction you want if you pick the right wind conditions.

As the burner heats the air it becomes less dense and rises. The hot air then shapes the balloon. Since the hot air is lighter and less dense than the air outside, it floats away and carries the balloon with it.

Making Hot Air

The burners are the balloon's engines. They burn propane gas to fill the balloon with hot air and make it rise. To stay aloft, the pilot keeps topping up with hot air. To descend, the air is allowed to cool, or let out through the top of the balloon.

Passengers and crew are carried in a light basket suspended beneath the balloon.

Airship

The difference between a balloon and an airship is not just the shape. An airship has engines, which means it can be flown in whatever direction you want. A century ago, vast airships carried passengers in luxury across the Atlantic.

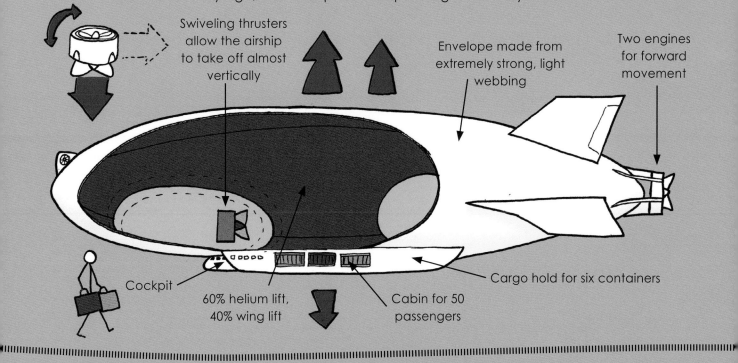

Swiveling thrusters allow the airship to take off almost vertically

Envelope made from extremely strong, light webbing

Two engines for forward movement

Cockpit

60% helium lift, 40% wing lift

Cabin for 50 passengers

Cargo hold for six containers

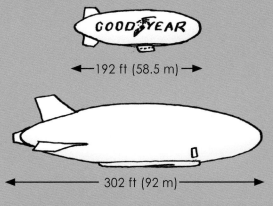

←192 ft (58.5 m)→

←302 ft (92 m)→

Airlander 10

The experimental Airlander 10 is an airship being built in the UK. When it is complete, it will be by far the largest aircraft in the world: 302 ft (92 m) long, 143 ft (43.5 m) wide, and 85 ft (26 m) tall. But that is small compared to the giant airship planned for the future, which the makers hope can help in survey work and disaster relief.

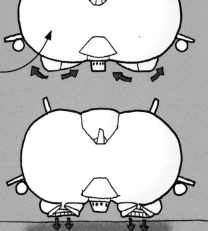

Not all the Airlander's lift comes from the lighter-than-air helium gas that fills its envelope. When full, it is shaped like a wing, and as the propellers drive it forward, the shape provides lift too.

Landing Cushion

The Airlander has no landing wheels. Instead it shoots out its own inflatable cushion for landing, along with jets of air. That means it can land anywhere, even on water.

Drones

You don't need a pilot to fly a plane. Drones, or Unmanned Aerial Vehicles (UAVs), are robot aircraft that can fly by themselves. Some don't even need a controller on the ground to send them instructions but are controlled by electronic programs.

Flying Eyes

Drones give a great bird's-eye view of inaccessible places, or places too dangerous for people to go. Many are basically flying cameras, used by police to track criminals, aid agencies to monitor disasters in dangerous conditions, and even film crews to shoot thrilling overhead views.

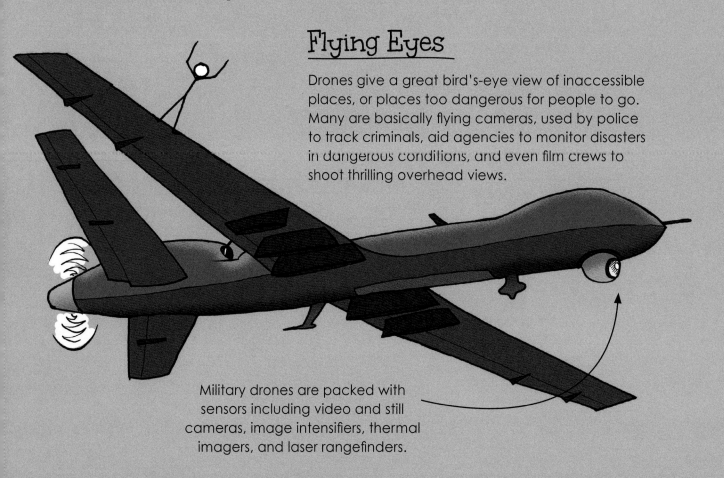

Military drones are packed with sensors including video and still cameras, image intensifiers, thermal imagers, and laser rangefinders.

Remote Control

Large sophisticated drones, such as those used by the military, need a crew of three on the ground: a pilot and two sensor operators. To fly the drone, the pilot moves a joystick just as if flying a real plane—but has to rely on a narrow camera view. If the drone is out of view, the signals are relayed to the drone via a satellite.

Quadcopters

While large military drones are more like ordinary planes with wings, most smaller drones are special kinds of helicopter called quadcopters. Quadcopters have not just one rotor but four.

In the future, you might receive deliveries wherever you are by drones that home in on your smartphone.

The quadcopter changes direction and height by varying the relative speed of the rotors.

Unlike ordinary helicopters, the pitch of the rotors on a quadcopter is fixed.

The speed of the four rotors is electronically co-ordinated.

Moving the control to the left increases the rotation of the right-hand rotors, so the quadcopter banks left.

A camera lets film-makers use drones for aerial views.

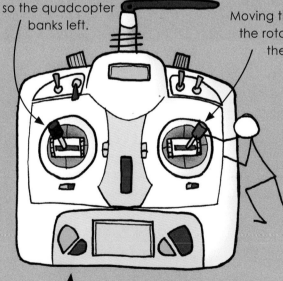

Moving the control to the right increases the rotation of the left-hand rotors, so the quadcopter banks right.

If the quadcopter is out of sight, it can be controlled with the aid of a virtual reality headset, which continually feeds the view seen by the drone's cameras.

Quadcopters for businesses, emergencies, and home use are operated by devices rather like games controllers. You can control some of the simplest quadcopters with just a smartphone.

Rockets

Getting things into space demands a huge amount of power—the kind of power only rockets can provide. Unlike jet and piston engines, rocket engines have few moving parts. They rely entirely on the massive force of expansion of burning rocket fuel.

Launch Stages

Most of a rocket's weight is fuel, and it uses most of it simply getting off the ground. So rather than carrying vast tanks with them for an entire journey, spacecraft are built in parts. After they are launched, rockets used for launching are jettisoned in stages.

3 Less than four minutes after launch and 100 miles (160 km) up, the main rockets have burned all their fuel and cut out. They too are jettisoned, and the second-stage rockets, a smaller version of the main rockets, fire up.

Payload

The payload is whatever the rocket is launching into space. It could be a satellite destined to orbit the Earth, or a space probe on a mission to distant planets. Or it could be a module carrying astronauts to a space station, or even further.

Fuel

Oxygen

Pumps and valves

Combustion chamber

2 Two minutes after launch and over 30 miles (8 km) up, the solid boosters cut out and fall away. The main rockets, powered by liquid fuel—liquid oxygen and hydrogen—fire to blast the spacecraft up to over 10,000 mph (16,000 km/h).

1 To give the kick it needs to take off from the launch pad, the spacecraft has solid rocket boosters strapped to the side. They use gunpowder-like solid fuel which burns ferociously but briefly.

A rocket is propelled by the reaction between the expanding gases and the body of the rocket.

At the top of the Space Launch System (SLS) is the Multi-Purpose Crew Vehicle in which astronauts will travel to the Moon or Mars. It consists of four parts:

4 The fairing (protective covering) for the payload falls away and after six minutes the second-stage rockets also burn out and fall away, leaving the payload to continue by itself.

Rocket for Deep space

It will take a hugely powerful rocket to launch a spacecraft big enough to carry astronauts as far as Mars. So NASA are developing their Space Launch System. It will be the most powerful rocket ever built, with five engines in its main stage.

Launch abort—an escape capsule for the crew if anything goes wrong early in the flight.

Crew module—the small conical compartment in which the astronauts travel. It's so tiny that the four-man crew have little room to move around.

Service module—this is where the works are: the engines, the solar panels that collect energy, and the crew's oxygen generator.

Adapter attaches the module to the booster

Rocket sizes

The biggest and most powerful rockets yet were the Saturn V rockets that launched the Apollo missions carrying men to the Moon between 1968 and 1972. Each was 363 ft (110 m) tall and blasted a payload of 260,000 lb (117,900 kg)—as much as 20 buses—up into space.

UNITED STATES

Passenger Ships

If one of the world's biggest passenger ships was stood on end, it would stretch almost to the top of New York's Empire State Building. They are like floating cities with theaters, swimming pools, streets, restaurants, and much more. Most are built for cruising at leisure from port to port. But the *Queen Mary 2* is designed as an ocean liner, carrying people in luxury across the Atlantic.

The Royal Court Theater

The Royal Court is a full-sized theater with 832 seats for the audience, including boxes, balconies, and a grand circle. Here you can see major productions of musicals and operas while cruising the high seas.

Passenger Cabins

The *Queen Mary 2* has over 1,000 cabins, which can take 2,620 passengers. Unlike earlier ocean liners, the *Queen Mary 2*'s passenger cabins are mostly in the ship's upper decks. That means that more than 800 of the cabins have their own private balcony, far above the waves.

There are 13 passenger decks and 17 decks overall.

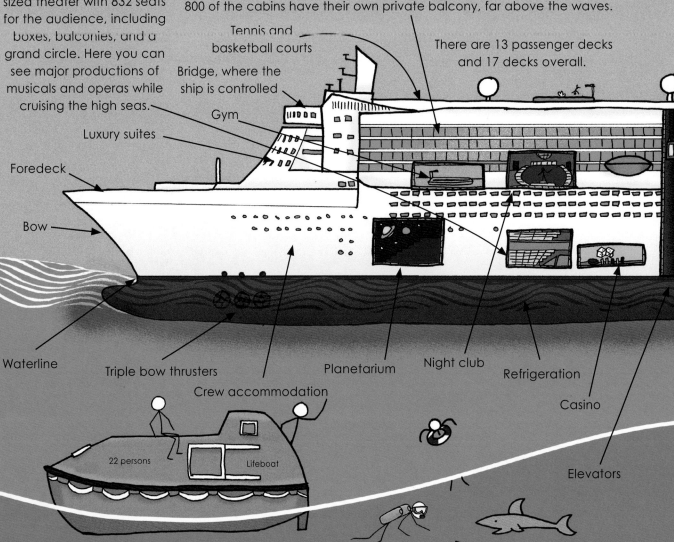

Tennis and basketball courts

Bridge, where the ship is controlled

Gym

Luxury suites

Foredeck

Bow

Waterline

Triple bow thrusters

Crew accommodation

Planetarium

Night club

Refrigeration

Casino

Elevators

22 persons   Lifeboat

To the lifeboats!

In case of emergency, *Queen Mary 2* has 22 Schat-Harding lifeboats hanging from davits (mini-cranes) that can be lowered in less than 30 seconds for an escape. All ships now have enough lifeboats on each side to take all the passengers and crew.

Port = the left of the ship, looking forward over the bow

Starboard = the right of the ship

Big Ship

The *Queen Mary 2* is enormous, weighing over 75,000 tons. It is 1,132 ft (345 m) long, and it would take you over ten minutes to walk from one end to the other. And, at 236 ft (72 m) high, it wouldn't fit under San Francisco's Golden Gate Bridge.

Engine Power

The *Queen Mary 2*'s power comes from four huge diesel engines in the engine room at the bottom of the ship, and two gas turbines at the top beneath the funnel. The engines don't drive the propellers directly. Instead they generate electricity to drive the electric motors outside the hull that do the actual propulsion. They also generate the power for the ship's electrical systems.

- Only the turbines are used near ports because they are less polluting.

- Out on the open ocean, the diesels fire up.

- Two of the *Queen Mary 2*'s propulsion units can swivel around to steer the ship, so there is no need for a rudder.

Booked

Near the front of the ship is a large wood-paneled library. There are over 6,000 books to choose from, to while away the voyage. It is the world's largest floating library.

Covered pool

Gas turbine generators

Funnel

Upper deck

Restaurants

Afterdeck

Electric drive units

Stern

Casino

Grand lobby

Flower stores

Hull

Electric drive units

Diesel/electric engines

Propellers

Propulsion units

Hydraulic Steering unit

Sea Grass

The games deck has courts for basketball and tennis, as well as gold simulators. There is even a lawn with real grass growing.

Bulbous Bow

Like many large oceangoing ships, the *Queen Mary 2* has a bulb extending in front of the bow below the waterline. This breaks up the water ahead of the bow and reduces the slowing effect of the water.

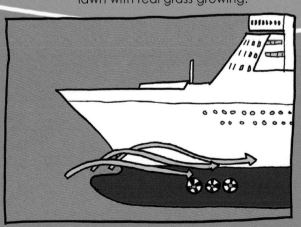

Engines and Propulsion

You can move a small boat along just by pulling on oars (rowboat) or using a sail to catch the wind (sailboat), but many small boats are driven by motors (motorboats)—and nearly all big ships are driven by powerful engines. Motors and engines move the boat by turning a propeller or blasting out a jet of water.

Hybrid Power

Big ships have big diesel engines or turbines in engine rooms deep inside the hull. Most engines still turn propeller shafts to drive the propellers outside the hull directly. But some ships, including the *Queen Mary 2*, have hybrid systems. These use diesel engines like power stations to drive electricity generators. The generators are wired up to electric motors outside the hull that drive the propellers directly.

The diesel engines burn diesel fuel to create power.

Each diesel engine drives an electricity generator to make electricity.

Screwy

A ship's propeller, or screw, works by moving water as it spins. Because the blades are twisted at an angle, they draw water in from the side, then push it out behind, pushing the boat along. Ship's propellers can run much, much slower than aircraft propellers because water is much, much denser than air.

Jet-Propelled

On jet skis and some other small boats, you can't see a propeller at all. Instead, the boat is driven along by a powerful whoosh of water. These pump-jet boats do still have a propeller, but it's called an impeller—and it's hidden inside a tube in the hull. The impeller draws in water through an intake, then shoots it out in a jet to drive the boat along.

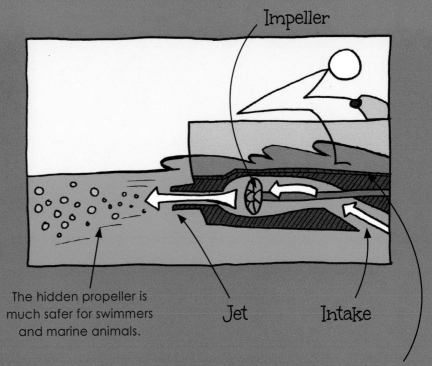

Impeller

The hidden propeller is much safer for swimmers and marine animals.

Jet

Intake

Pump-jets are much quieter than ordinary propellers

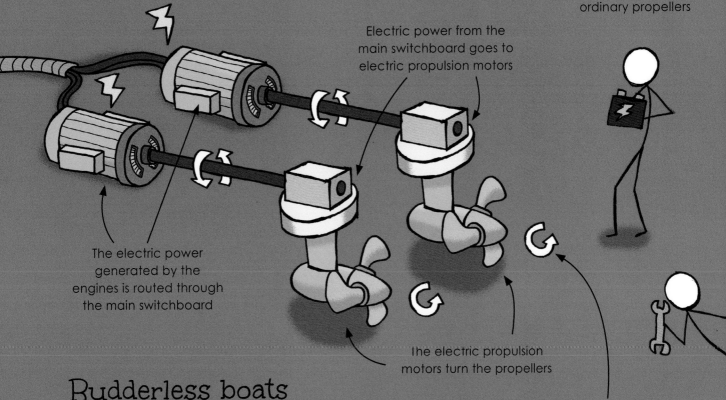

Electric power from the main switchboard goes to electric propulsion motors

The electric power generated by the engines is routed through the main switchboard

The electric propulsion motors turn the propellers

The whirling of the propellers drives the ship forward as they push water out of the way

Rudderless boats

Some electric propulsion motors, called azimuth thrusters, can be swiveled in almost any direction. That means the ship can be propelled in almost any direction, which makes it much more manoeuvrable in tight situations. And there is no need for a rudder at all.

Hulls and Hydrofoils

A boat's hull is the part that sits in the water and keeps the boat afloat. It doesn't sit on top of the water but sinks a little way in, and as it does, it pushes water out of the way—but the water pushes back. Because the hull is hollow, it is actually quite light compared to the weight of water pushed out of the way. So all that weight of water pushing back is enough to keep the boat floating.

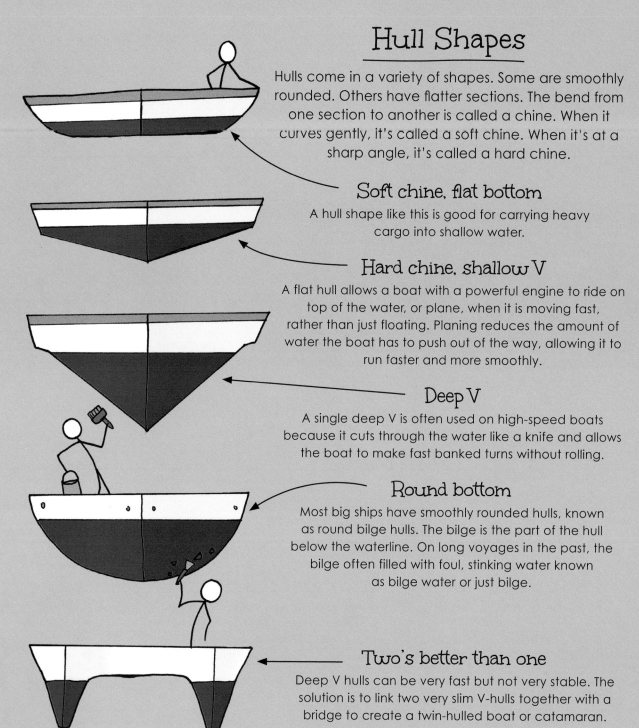

Hull Shapes

Hulls come in a variety of shapes. Some are smoothly rounded. Others have flatter sections. The bend from one section to another is called a chine. When it curves gently, it's called a soft chine. When it's at a sharp angle, it's called a hard chine.

Soft chine, flat bottom

A hull shape like this is good for carrying heavy cargo into shallow water.

Hard chine, shallow V

A flat hull allows a boat with a powerful engine to ride on top of the water, or plane, when it is moving fast, rather than just floating. Planing reduces the amount of water the boat has to push out of the way, allowing it to run faster and more smoothly.

Deep V

A single deep V is often used on high-speed boats because it cuts through the water like a knife and allows the boat to make fast banked turns without rolling.

Round bottom

Most big ships have smoothly rounded hulls, known as round bilge hulls. The bilge is the part of the hull below the waterline. On long voyages in the past, the bilge often filled with foul, stinking water known as bilge water or just bilge.

Two's better than one

Deep V hulls can be very fast but not very stable. The solution is to link two very slim V-hulls together with a bridge to create a twin-hulled boat or catamaran.

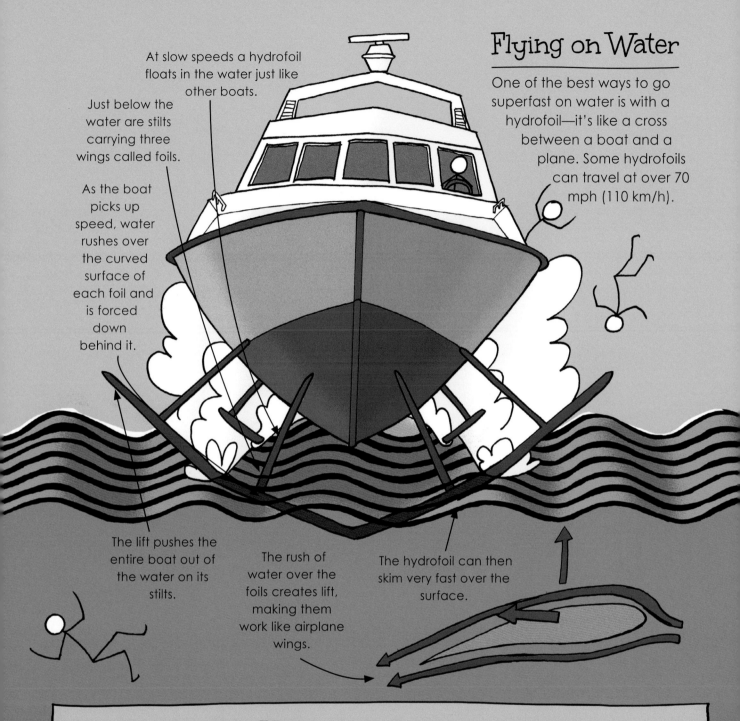

At slow speeds a hydrofoil floats in the water just like other boats.

Just below the water are stilts carrying three wings called foils.

As the boat picks up speed, water rushes over the curved surface of each foil and is forced down behind it.

Flying on Water

One of the best ways to go superfast on water is with a hydrofoil—it's like a cross between a boat and a plane. Some hydrofoils can travel at over 70 mph (110 km/h).

The lift pushes the entire boat out of the water on its stilts.

The rush of water over the foils creates lift, making them work like airplane wings.

The hydrofoil can then skim very fast over the surface.

The Keel

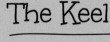

Every boat has a backbone, known as the keel, running from front to back at the bottom of the boat. Boatbuilding always starts with the laying down of the keel. Then ribs are attached to the keel, and planks or plates are laid over the ribs to create the hull.

On some boats, especially sailing boats, the keel extends to form a fin to help stop the boat rolling over (*above left*).

In modern steel boats, the ribs extend across the hull as thick walls, known as bulkheads, which not only give the hull extra strength but stop water from filling the entire hull if it should spring a leak.

Aircraft Carriers

The flight deck of a big aircraft carrier is a noisy, dangerous, and exciting place. When a major mission is on, there is an incredible din from the roar of the jets. Every 25 seconds, a plane is loaded into the catapult, shot along the deck and out over the sea—and, with luck, away . . .

Flight deck

The top of an aircraft carrier is almost entirely flight deck— —a vast flat space for the planes to take off and land. On a big US Navy carrier, the deck is often almost as long as the Empire State Building is high (over 1,000 ft /300 m), and a football pitch would nearly fit across it (300 ft/ 90 m)!

Radar systems

An aircraft carrier doesn't just need the radar and other equipment that ordinary ships use for navigation. It must have all the systems for tracking and guiding dozens of planes in the air. It also has to monitor enemy activity. So the tops of the ship's islands (operational towers) bristle with an array of radar and communications antennae.

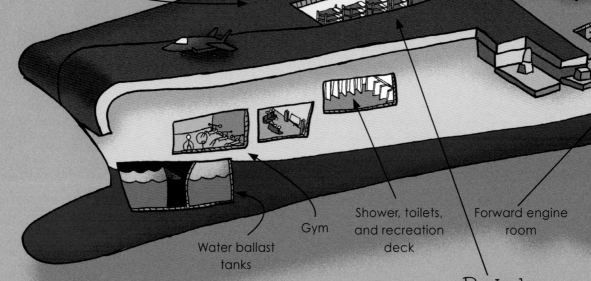

Lift

Bridge

Gym

Water ballast tanks

Shower, toilets, and recreation deck

Forward engine room

Sling shot

Despite its length, the flight deck is not long enough for a normal takeoff. So planes are given a kick-start with a catapult wire attached to the nose. High-pressure steam pistons fling the plane up to 165 mph (265 km/h) in just two seconds before the wires are dropped and the plane takes off.

Racked up

Ordinary crew members don't have their own bedrooms. They have to share a compartment with about 60 other people, all sleeping in single bunks. The bunks are called racks because they're crammed together in stacks of three.

The islands

There's very little superstructure on a carrier—just the two islands. The ship is controlled from the tower at the front. This is where the captain is in charge. The rear island is the flight control for the planes. Here the air boss rules the roost.

Air traffic control

Jet blast deflector used during takeoff

Hooked

The flight deck isn't actually long enough for a landing. So planes have a hook dangling from the tail. It's the pilot's tricky task to catch the hook on arrestor wires stretched across the deck when coming in to land. That way the plane will be brought to a halt before shooting off the other end of the deck!

Some fighter planes can take off or land vertically, without using arrestor wires

Rudder

Officers' quarters

The officers live in slightly more spacious rooms at the rear of the ship.

Propeller

Senior ratings' dining room

Stabilizer

Water tanks

Aft engine rooms

Catering

Hospital

Aircraft carriers may be involved in combat, so most have full-sized hospitals to cope with casualties. A typical carrier has a hospital with 50 or more beds, several operating rooms, and intensive care units.

Hangar deck

There's only room for a few planes up on deck. Most planes are stored down on the hangar deck when not in use. It's two decks down and absolutely vast. On a big carrier, 60 or more planes may be lined up here, ready to be moved to one of the four giant lifts to the flight deck.

The Crew

It takes a lot of people to run a carrier. There are 2,500 men and women who fly and maintain the aircraft and over 3,000 more to keep the ship running. That means the galleys have to serve 18,000 meals a day to keep them fed!

Help, I'm Lost!

With thousands of compartments and numerous decks, it's easy to get lost on a carrier. So on some, every sailor has a phone app to show exactly where he or she is!

Cargo Ships

The world's largest container ship, the MSC *Oscar*, is ginormous. It weighs nearly 200,000 tons. Stand it on end, and it would reach much higher even than London's Shard skyscraper. And it can carry 19,224 containers. It could carry enough new washing machines to give one to every single home in Los Angeles!

What are Containers?

Containers are standard-sized steel boxes for carrying cargo. They come in 20-ft (6-m) and 40-ft (12-m) versions. As they're all the same size, they can be loaded and unloaded by the same cranes anywhere and stacked up like vast brick walls.

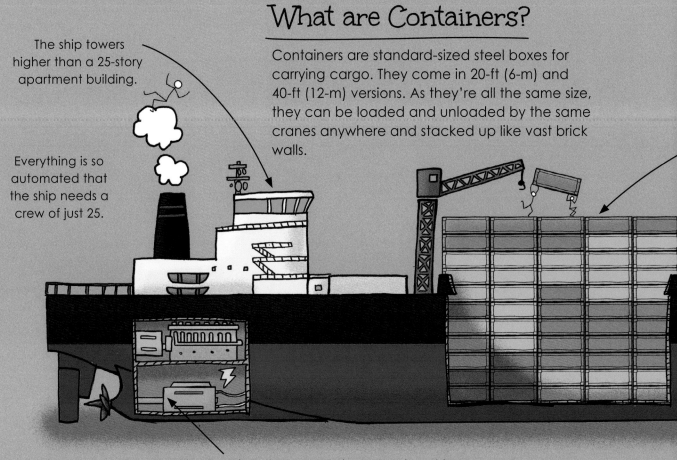

The ship towers higher than a 25-story apartment building.

Everything is so automated that the ship needs a crew of just 25.

The diesel engines that power giant container ships are the largest engines ever built.

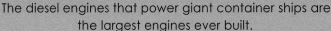

TEUs means "twenty-foot equivalent units"—the number of containers a ship can carry

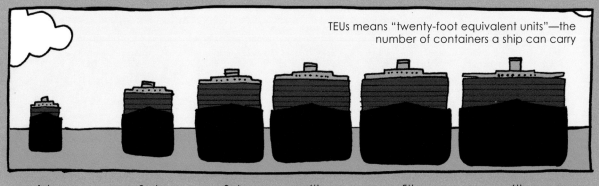

1st Generation pre 1960–1970 500–800 TEUs	2nd Generation 1971–1980 1,000–2,500 TEUs	3rd Generation 1980–1988 3,000–4,000 TEUs	4th Generation 1988–2000 4,000–5,000 TEUs	5th Generation 2000–2005 5,000–8,000 TEUs	6th Generation 2006–2015 11,000–14,500 TEUs

Ship to Truck

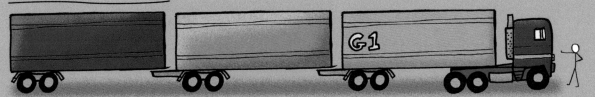

Trucks and trains are built to take containers exactly as they are. So cranes can simply whirl the containers off a ship and on to a truck. There's no need to open them at all. Computerized numbering is vital for keeping track of them, though!

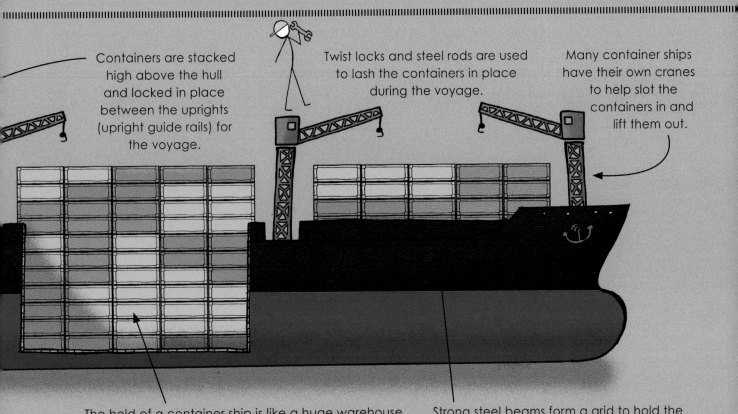

Containers are stacked high above the hull and locked in place between the uprights (upright guide rails) for the voyage.

Twist locks and steel rods are used to lash the containers in place during the voyage.

Many container ships have their own cranes to help slot the containers in and lift them out.

The hold of a container ship is like a huge warehouse divided into cells separated by upright guide rails.

Strong steel beams form a grid to hold the ship together, with all the weight it's carrying.

Container Generations

The first container ships appeared in 1956 and could carry fewer than 1,000 containers. Since then they've got bigger and bigger and bigger... For a while until 1985, shipbuilders were limited by the size of ship that could fit through the Panama Canal. Then they decided it was better to build vast and take the long route around South America. The 7th generation ships now being built may carry up to 30,000 containers!

Bulk Carriers

"Bulk" means loose and liquid materials, such as iron ore or oil. These don't need containers; they can simply be poured into the ship's hold or tank. Oil tankers built in the 1970s, known as supertankers, were the largest ships ever built. Some were over 1,500 ft (450 m) long and weighed 350,000 tons. They could each carry 60 million gallons (272 million liters) of crude oil—enough to supply the entire UK for well over a day.

Sailing Boats

For many people, nothing can beat the sheer thrill of being driven along by the wind alone in a yacht or a sailing dinghy. Using the wind to push the boat in the direction you want to go requires considerable skill, but that's what makes it so fun.

Wind-Driven

Many large sailing ships in the past had square sails set across the ship at right angles. With these, the ship was simply blown along in front of the wind. But the triangular sails on yachts work differently. They are in line with the boat, not across it, and the sail functions like an aircraft's wing.

Raised pressure

As the wind blows over the sail, the sail bows out.

The flow of air over the curved sail creates a sideways force, just as an aircraft's wings create lift.

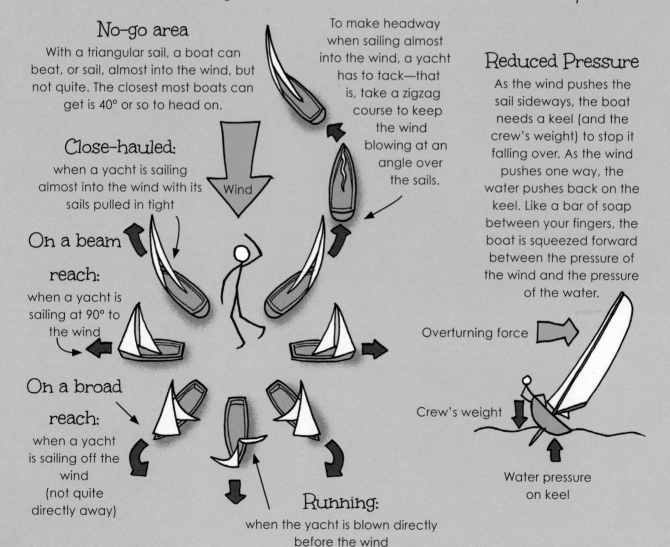

No-go area

With a triangular sail, a boat can beat, or sail, almost into the wind, but not quite. The closest most boats can get is 40° or so to head on.

Close-hauled:

when a yacht is sailing almost into the wind with its sails pulled in tight

On a beam reach:

when a yacht is sailing at 90° to the wind

On a broad reach:

when a yacht is sailing off the wind (not quite directly away)

To make headway when sailing almost into the wind, a yacht has to tack—that is, take a zigzag course to keep the wind blowing at an angle over the sails.

Wind

Running:

when the yacht is blown directly before the wind

Reduced Pressure

As the wind pushes the sail sideways, the boat needs a keel (and the crew's weight) to stop it falling over. As the wind pushes one way, the water pushes back on the keel. Like a bar of soap between your fingers, the boat is squeezed forward between the pressure of the wind and the pressure of the water.

Overturning force

Crew's weight

Water pressure on keel

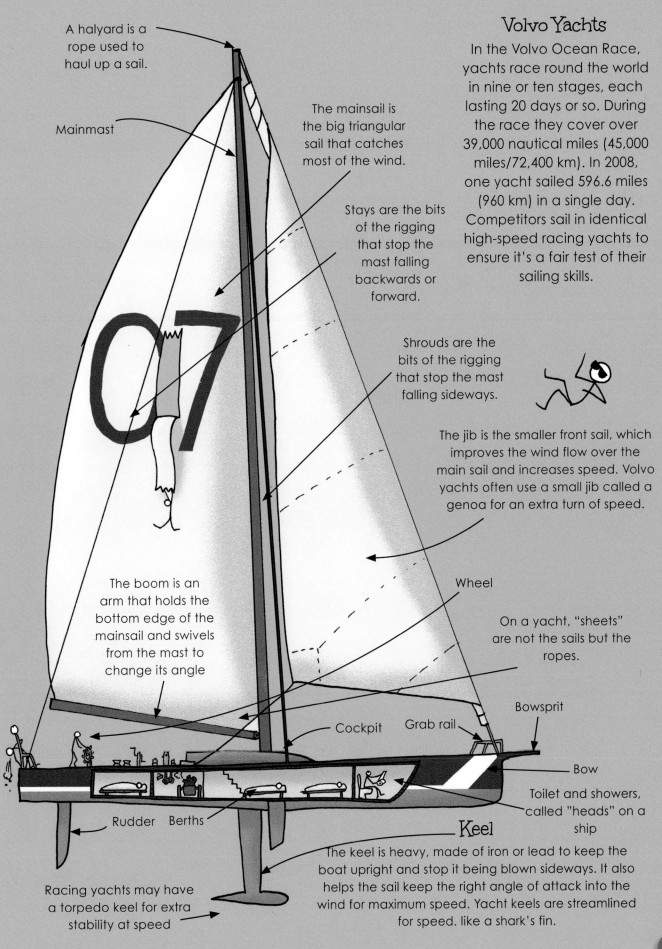

A halyard is a rope used to haul up a sail.

Mainmast

The mainsail is the big triangular sail that catches most of the wind.

Stays are the bits of the rigging that stop the mast falling backwards or forward.

Shrouds are the bits of the rigging that stop the mast falling sideways.

Volvo Yachts

In the Volvo Ocean Race, yachts race round the world in nine or ten stages, each lasting 20 days or so. During the race they cover over 39,000 nautical miles (45,000 miles/72,400 km). In 2008, one yacht sailed 596.6 miles (960 km) in a single day. Competitors sail in identical high-speed racing yachts to ensure it's a fair test of their sailing skills.

The jib is the smaller front sail, which improves the wind flow over the main sail and increases speed. Volvo yachts often use a small jib called a genoa for an extra turn of speed.

The boom is an arm that holds the bottom edge of the mainsail and swivels from the mast to change its angle

Wheel

On a yacht, "sheets" are not the sails but the ropes.

Cockpit

Grab rail

Bowsprit

Bow

Rudder   Berths

Toilet and showers, called "heads" on a ship

Keel

The keel is heavy, made of iron or lead to keep the boat upright and stop it being blown sideways. It also helps the sail keep the right angle of attack into the wind for maximum speed. Yacht keels are streamlined for speed. like a shark's fin.

Racing yachts may have a torpedo keel for extra stability at speed

Submarines

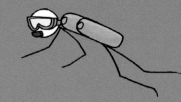

Modern nuclear submarines are the most secretive craft on Earth. They can dive at least 800 ft (240 m) down and travel at almost 30 mph (50 km/h). They can stay submerged continuously for three months, during which time they could travel almost twice round the world. They can go anywhere, and because they're hidden beneath the water, no one ever knows where they are.

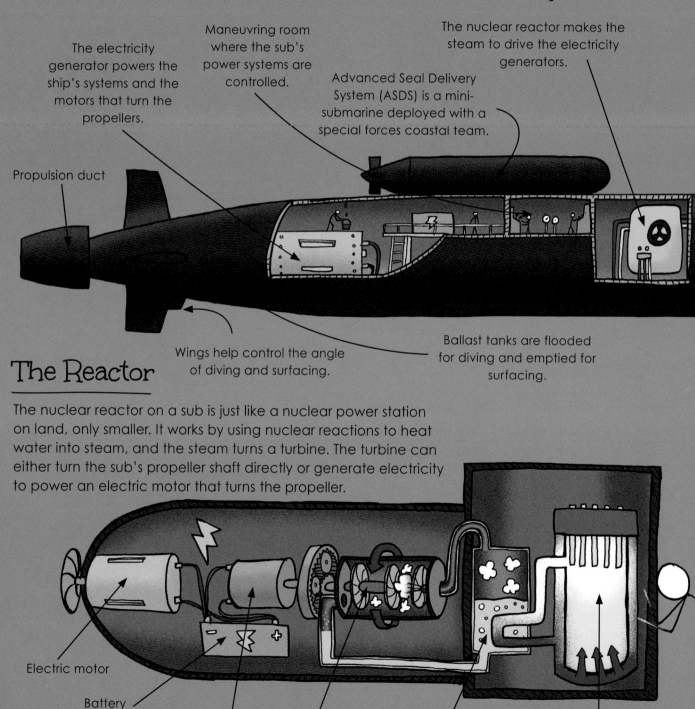

The electricity generator powers the ship's systems and the motors that turn the propellers.

Maneuvring room where the sub's power systems are controlled.

The nuclear reactor makes the steam to drive the electricity generators.

Advanced Seal Delivery System (ASDS) is a mini-submarine deployed with a special forces coastal team.

Propulsion duct

Wings help control the angle of diving and surfacing.

Ballast tanks are flooded for diving and emptied for surfacing.

The Reactor

The nuclear reactor on a sub is just like a nuclear power station on land, only smaller. It works by using nuclear reactions to heat water into steam, and the steam turns a turbine. The turbine can either turn the sub's propeller shaft directly or generate electricity to power an electric motor that turns the propeller.

Electric motor

Battery

Electricity generator

Turbine

Steam generator

Nuclear reactor

Diesel v Nuclear

Submarines powered by diesel engines can only stay underwater for a few days. That's because diesel engines need air to work. So once a diesel sub's submerged it runs on battery-powered electric motors, which need recharging at the surface after a few days. Diesel fuel is also very bulky, so a diesel submarine can only carry enough fuel to last a few weeks.

Nuclear subs are very expensive to build. But nuclear reactors give power without any air, and the fuel they need is so concentrated that a nuclear submarine could sail for years without refuelling. The only reason a nuclear sub has to come up after 90 days is because the crew get hungry.

Cramped crew quarters, where the submariners sleep in bunks when not on duty

The command center, where the officers see what's going on up top on big screens fed by fiber-optic systems from the surface

Masts

Conning tower

Missile tubes for launching missiles straight up

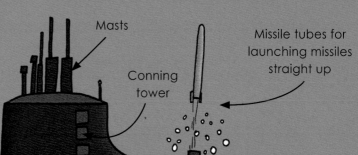

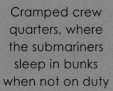

Missile room, where missiles are stored ready for loading into tubes

Missiles are fired from missile tubes at the front.

Retractable bow planes, together with the wings at the rear of the submarine, control the submarine's depth.

Sonar for detecting other submarines and obstacles underwater

Vent lets air out to allow the tanks to be filled with water for diving.

Trim tanks at either end are filled with water or emptied to keep the submarine level.

Wings on the side of the sub control the diving angle.

Going Down!

The key to a sub's ability to dive and surface is its double skin. In between the inner and the outer skin are large spaces that can hold water, called ballast tanks. To dive, the sub pumps water in to flood these tanks, making the sub heavy enough to sink. To surface, it simply pumps the water out again.

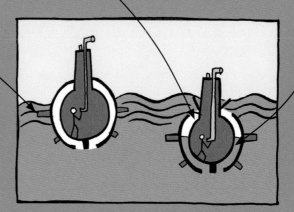

Deep Diver

Submarines can go down only about 1,000 ft (300 m). Yet the deepest part of the ocean is almost 36,000 ft (10,900 m) deep. To explore this far, you need a very special craft. Amazingly, in 1960 Jacques Piccard and Don Walsh made it to the very bottom in the bathyscaphe *Trieste*. To repeat this feat in 2012, filmmaker James Cameron used the remarkable submersible, *Deepsea Challenger*.

What is a Submersible?

Submarines can operate entirely by themselves. Submersibles are small underwater craft that need a support crew on the surface to control them, or supply power or air. The best-known submersible is the ocean research vessel *Alvin*, which has been carrying researchers into the deep for more than half a century.

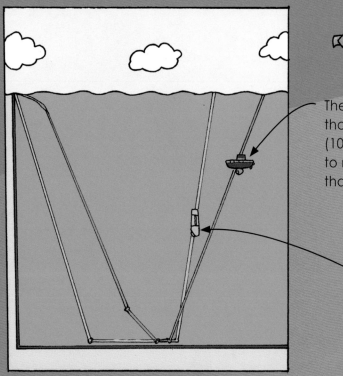

The *Trieste* actually got even deeper than *Deepsea Challenger*, at 35,814 ft (10,916 m) down, but it took five hours to make the descent and spent less than 20 minutes down there.

It took Cameron's *Deepsea Challenger* 2 hours, 37 minutes to plunge all the way down to the bottom. He reached a maximum depth of 35,787 ft (10,908 m) and spent three hours there filming there, before resurfacing in less than an hour.

Voyage to the Bottom

The Challenger Deep is the deepest part of the deepest trench in the ocean—the Mariana Trench, off the Mariana Islands in the western Pacific Ocean.

Deepsea Challenger

Down she goes

Deepsea Challenger is lowered by cable from the support boat *Mermaid Sapphire*, which provides continual support and keeps in touch with the pilot through wires.

Ocean bath foam

Deepsea Challenger's body is carved out of a material called syntactic foam. Superlight yet stronger than steel, it not only helps the sub float back up, but provides a structure strong enough to take the incredible pressures of the deep ocean. It is made from millions of hollow glass microspheres suspended in an epoxy resin.

Light in the darkness

It's pitch dark deep down in the ocean, so for Cameron to film, the sub needs lots of lights. Besides individual search lights, the sub has an eight-foot bank of superbright LEDS angled down to flood the sea floor with light.

Battery

The power for all the life support, lighting and camera systems comes from 70 bread loaf-sized batteries in plastic boxes on the sub's sides.

The pilot ball

The pilot is cocooned inside a tiny sphere barely 3 ft (1 m) across and has to sit with his knees scrunched up for the entire voyage. It's round because a sphere is the best shape for standing up to the huge pressures of the ocean deep.

Stabilizer fin

Hard point where a crane can grab the sub

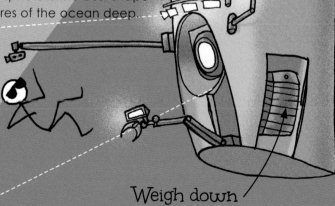

Weigh down

To pull it down to the ocean bottom, the sub has over 1,000 lb (454 kg) of solid steel plates stuck to the side by electromagnetism. To surface, the pilot simply flips a switch to turn off the electromagnets. The steel plates drop off, and the light foam body sends the sub shooting up.

Hovercraft

If you really want to ride on air, you need a hovercraft. This craft glides on a cushion of air and is also called an Air Cushion Vehicle, or ACV. It can travel on water and land equally easily, and it is used by the military as well as in rescue missions. The largest is the 187-ft (57-m) Russian Zubr.

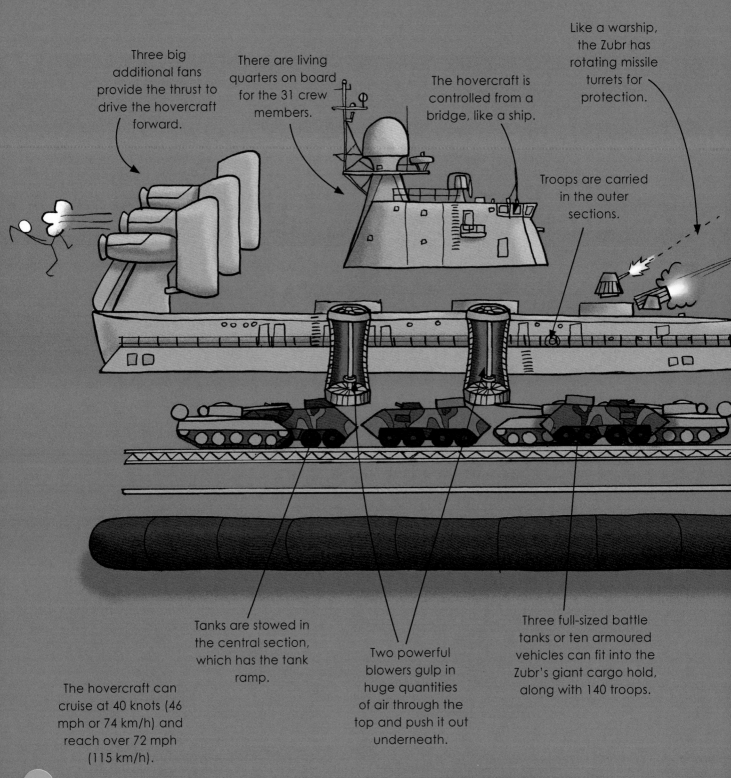

Three big additional fans provide the thrust to drive the hovercraft forward.

There are living quarters on board for the 31 crew members.

The hovercraft is controlled from a bridge, like a ship.

Like a warship, the Zubr has rotating missile turrets for protection.

Troops are carried in the outer sections.

Tanks are stowed in the central section, which has the tank ramp.

The hovercraft can cruise at 40 knots (46 mph or 74 km/h) and reach over 72 mph (115 km/h).

Two powerful blowers gulp in huge quantities of air through the top and push it out underneath.

Three full-sized battle tanks or ten armoured vehicles can fit into the Zubr's giant cargo hold, along with 140 troops.

How Hovercraft Work

Hovercraft have powerful fans that draw air in through the top and out underneath. A fabric skirt around the edge of the bottom traps the blown air under the craft to create the cushion that lifts the craft.

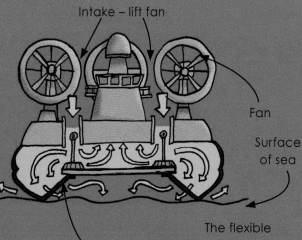

Intake – lift fan

Fan

Surface of sea

The flexible skirt allows the hovercraft to ride over obstacles.

Some air escapes

An additional fan pushes air backwards to drive the hovercraft forward.

Cockpit

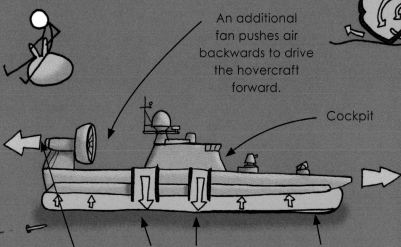

Air blows downwards

An air cushion inside the skirt supports the craft

A rudder behind the fan directs the air to steer the craft.

Useful Machines

The first hovercraft was invented in the 1950s by British engineer Christopher Cockerell. They are now used all around the world for everything from disaster relief to surveys, with mini versions raced as a sport.

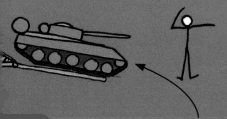

When the Zubr's ramp comes down, the tanks and troops can be out and into battle in minutes.

Zubr Craft

Because the Russian Zubr can zoom from water to land without stopping, it's perfect for a rapid invasion from the sea. It has not yet been used in battle.

Construction Cranes

Right now, scores of buildings more than 1,000 ft (300 m) tall are going up in cities all over the world. To build them, they need cranes that are just as tall—the tallest ever built. And these cranes don't just need to be tall. They have to lift very heavy weights and maneuver them to exactly where they are needed. This high up, even a small error could be disastrous.

Operator's cab

A crane operator's job is a tough one. You really need a head for heights. You have to be in shape too. Every morning you climb vertical ladders all the way up to the cab and, usually, drop in through the roof. Once inside, you'll be there all day—until you climb all the way back down again.

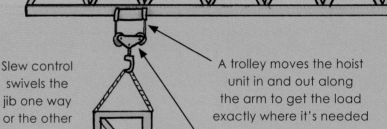

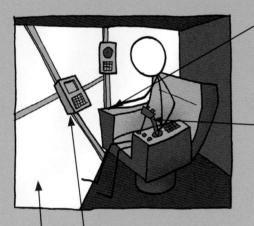

Slew control swivels the jib one way or the other

Hoist control lever starts the hoist winding up or down

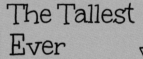

A trolley moves the hoist unit in and out along the arm to get the load exactly where it's needed

The hook that lifts the load is attached to the hoist unit

Hoist unit

Computer screen shows the weight of the load, the climb speed, wind speed, and much more

Electronic systems ensure the load and hoist speed are perfectly matched

Video systems give the operator a close-up view of the hook and load

Windows are made of laminated safety glass

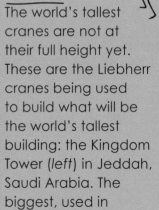

The Tallest Ever

The world's tallest cranes are not at their full height yet. These are the Liebherr cranes being used to build what will be the world's tallest building: the Kingdom Tower (*left*) in Jeddah, Saudi Arabia. The biggest, used in constructing the central tower, is a climbing crane, which means it will extend as the building rises, using it as support. The last section of crane, for lifting the top of the building into place, will be over 3,280 ft (1,000 m) up! Yet it will still only be 8 ft (2.4 m) wide.

The jib is the long arm that carries the load.

The load is hoisted by a powerful electric motor or winch that winds a strong metal cable in or out.

Balancing act

Lifting a load on a crane is a careful balancing act. There has to be a counterweight of concrete blocks on the end of the machinery arm, opposite the jib, to balance out the load. The crane's motors also add to the counterweight.

Cab

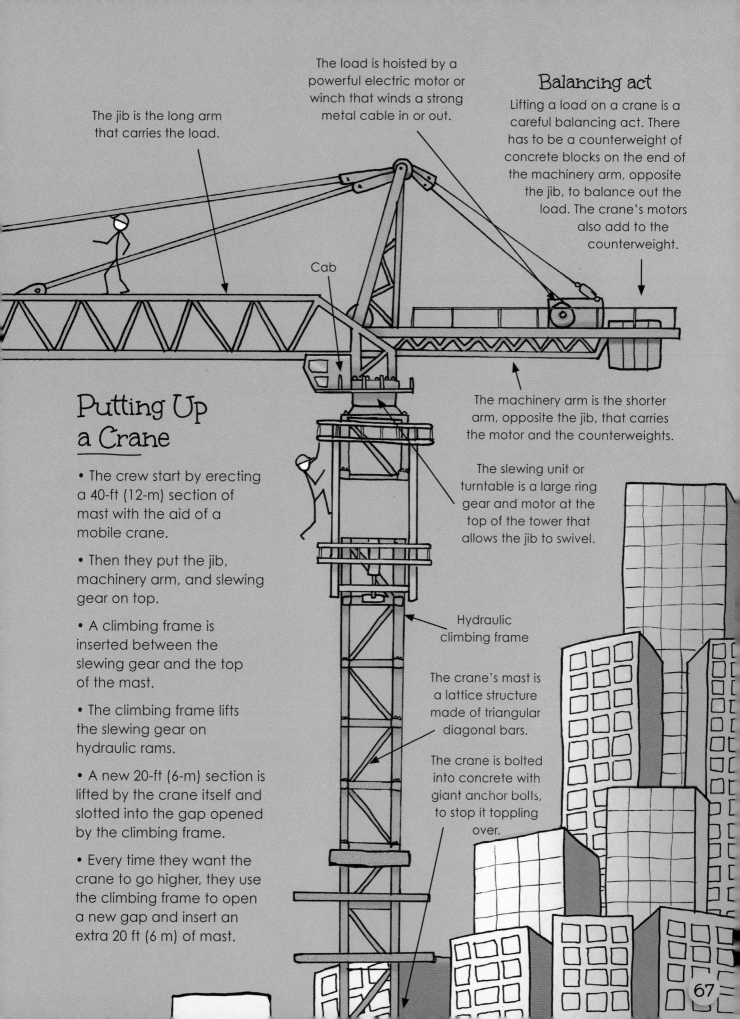

Putting Up a Crane

• The crew start by erecting a 40-ft (12-m) section of mast with the aid of a mobile crane.

• Then they put the jib, machinery arm, and slewing gear on top.

• A climbing frame is inserted between the slewing gear and the top of the mast.

• The climbing frame lifts the slewing gear on hydraulic rams.

• A new 20-ft (6-m) section is lifted by the crane itself and slotted into the gap opened by the climbing frame.

• Every time they want the crane to go higher, they use the climbing frame to open a new gap and insert an extra 20 ft (6 m) of mast.

The machinery arm is the shorter arm, opposite the jib, that carries the motor and the counterweights.

The slewing unit or turntable is a large ring gear and motor at the top of the tower that allows the jib to swivel.

Hydraulic climbing frame

The crane's mast is a lattice structure made of triangular diagonal bars.

The crane is bolted into concrete with giant anchor bolts, to stop it toppling over.

Dump Trucks

Mining companies need huge quantities of rocks moved fast—and the best way to do this is with giant dump trucks, sometimes called haul trucks. These big-as-a-house mine monsters never have to go on the road, so there is no limit to size—the bigger the better. All that matters is moving loads of rubble, fast. But mines are very tough, too. So these trucks have to be supertough.

Brute force

The powerhouse of a haul truck has to be unstoppable. That's why trucks like the BelAZ 75710 have two engines, not one, and they are both 16-cylinder diesels. The engines are simply electricity generators which produce the electricity to drive hugely powerful electric motors on four of the wheels, turning them directly.

The cab

The driver's cab is so small compared to the truck you can barely see it—and to reach it, the driver has to climb a ladder. The driver, of course, has power-assisted steering to steer those mighty wheels!

Turning tight

The truck has to make turns in tight places, so the front wheels can swivel a long way. That means a haul truck like the BelAZ 75710 can turn completely around in its own length.

The tipper

To empty the load, the front end of the hopper is powered up by massive hydraulic rams. When raised, the top of the hopper is higher than a five-story building!

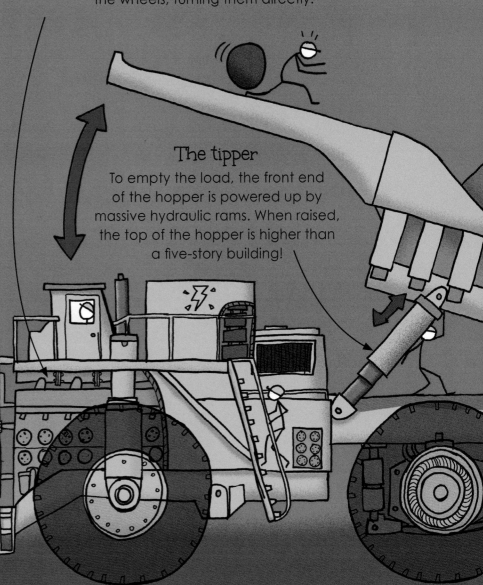

Big Digger

Haul trucks often get their load direct from another huge machine, a mechanical digger. This is like a giant spade that digs out the ground with a bucket moved by a hinged arm. The arm gets its power from hydraulic (fluid-filled) pistons. The digging arm and cabin are on a swiveling turntable, so it can be easily maneuverd.

High and Mighty

Right now, the biggest dump truck in the world is the BelAZ 75710 made in Belarus. It can move more than 450 tons of rubble in a single load. That's the weight of 250 or so cars or 40 African elephants! To shift all that weight, it has an engine with a torque (turning force) of 13,738 lb–ft—about 24 times that of a 2014 Formula One racing car!

How much?

If you wanted to buy a BelAZ 75710, it would cost you a cool $6,000,000 . . .

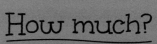

The hopper

The load is carried in the truck's hopper which is made from massively thick steel to take the weight and the constant battering of rubble. The hopper is filled up by mechanical diggers or an overhead conveyor. But it needs to be unloaded instantly. That's why the hopper is designed to tip up, so the load can slide straight out.

Big wheels

Monster dump trucks run on what may be the world's biggest wheels. They're typically taller than an African elephant—about the height of two tall adults put together. And there are usually six or eight of them—each with absolutely massive rubber tires. Those tires are supremely tough and chunky—you don't want a flat with one of these!

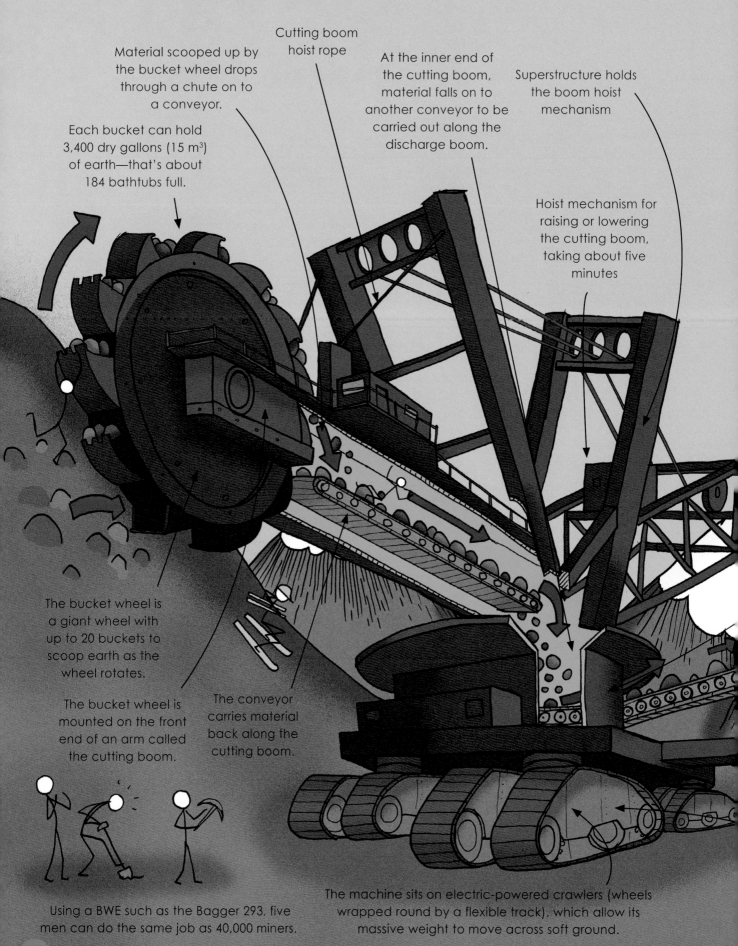

Cutting boom
hoist rope

Material scooped up by
the bucket wheel drops
through a chute on to
a conveyor.

At the inner end of
the cutting boom,
material falls on to
another conveyor to be
carried out along the
discharge boom.

Superstructure holds
the boom hoist
mechanism

Each bucket can hold
3,400 dry gallons (15 m³)
of earth—that's about
184 bathtubs full.

Hoist mechanism for
raising or lowering
the cutting boom,
taking about five
minutes

The bucket wheel is
a giant wheel with
up to 20 buckets to
scoop earth as the
wheel rotates.

The bucket wheel is
mounted on the front
end of an arm called
the cutting boom.

The conveyor
carries material
back along the
cutting boom.

Using a BWE such as the Bagger 293, five
men can do the same job as 40,000 miners.

The machine sits on electric-powered crawlers (wheels
wrapped round by a flexible track), which allow its
massive weight to move across soft ground.

Bucket Wheel Excavators

Gigantic bucket wheel excavators (BWEs) are the world's most monstrous vehicles. With their whirling bucket wheels, they can chew through the ground at a furious rate. The biggest can shift hundreds of thousands of tons of ground material, carving a deep gouge in the earth.

Big Bagger

The biggest BWE, and the biggest vehicle ever, is the Bagger 293, which mines brown coal near Hambach in Germany. It's 738 ft (225 m) long and 315 ft (96 m) tall—much longer and almost as tall as St Paul's Cathedral in London. It also weighs a crushing 14,200 tons! And it's got wheels, or rather, crawlers.

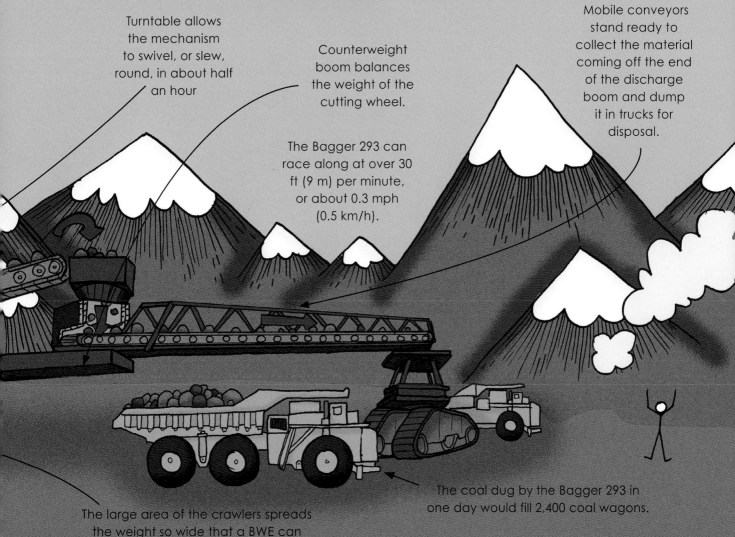

Turntable allows the mechanism to swivel, or slew, round, in about half an hour

Counterweight boom balances the weight of the cutting wheel.

Mobile conveyors stand ready to collect the material coming off the end of the discharge boom and dump it in trucks for disposal.

The Bagger 293 can race along at over 30 ft (9 m) per minute, or about 0.3 mph (0.5 km/h).

The large area of the crawlers spreads the weight so wide that a BWE can move over grass without damaging it.

The coal dug by the Bagger 293 in one day would fill 2,400 coal wagons.

Tunneling Machines

If you want to dig a really big tunnel, you need a boring machine—a tunnel boring machine ,or TBM. These are like gigantic drills that bore through the ground, leaving a complete tunnel behind them. Without them, city metro systems, water mains and road and other tunnels could not have been built.

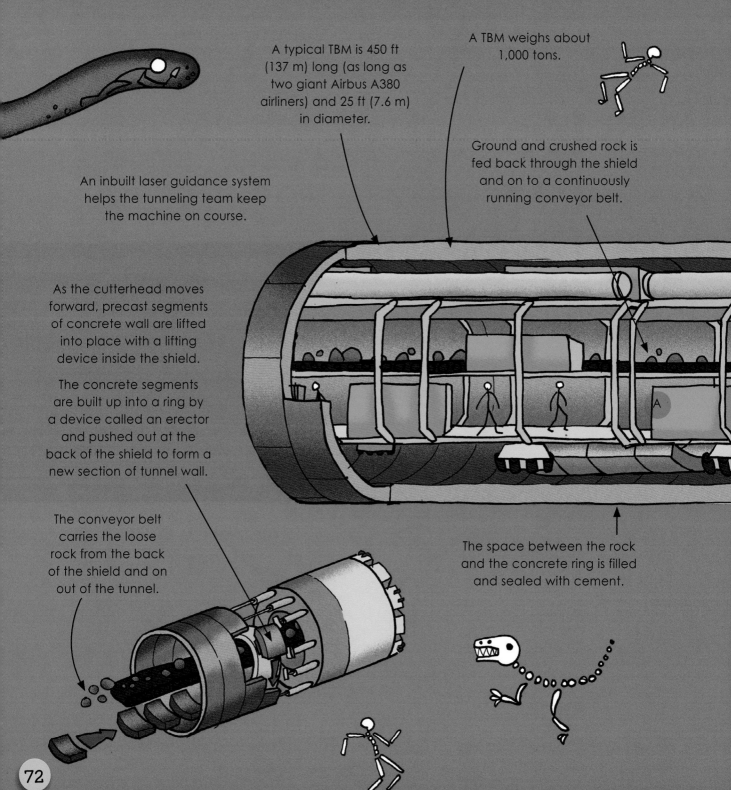

A typical TBM is 450 ft (137 m) long (as long as two giant Airbus A380 airliners) and 25 ft (7.6 m) in diameter.

A TBM weighs about 1,000 tons.

An inbuilt laser guidance system helps the tunneling team keep the machine on course.

Ground and crushed rock is fed back through the shield and on to a continuously running conveyor belt.

As the cutterhead moves forward, precast segments of concrete wall are lifted into place with a lifting device inside the shield.

The concrete segments are built up into a ring by a device called an erector and pushed out at the back of the shield to form a new section of tunnel wall.

The conveyor belt carries the loose rock from the back of the shield and on out of the tunnel.

The space between the rock and the concrete ring is filled and sealed with cement.

Workers' break room

The TBM needs only a small team, and the operator controlling the cutterhead sits some way behind in a control booth, monitoring progress on screens fed by cameras at the head.

The electric and hydraulic power systems are behind the cutter.

Pressure sensors continually monitor the turning power of the cutterhead and adjustments are made automatically.

The front of the TBM is a cylinder called a shield because it shields the tunnelers as they dig.

The cutterhead is driven round by powerful electric motors and grinds away the rock.

Powerful hydraulic rams press the cutterhead up against the rock face.

The front of the shield is a giant disc facing into the new rock. It's called the cutterhead and is fitted with incredibly tough steel cutting edges and scrapers.

Big Bertha Gets stuck

North America's biggest borer is Big Bertha, named after the US's first female mayor, Bertha Knight Landes, who was mayor of Seattle in the 1920s. Big Bertha weighs 7,000 tons and has a cutterhead 57.5 ft (17.5 m) in diameter. In 2013, it began drilling a massive double-decker highway tunnel in Seattle, cutting through 30 ft (9 m) of solid rock every day. But after 1,000 ft (300 m), it ground to a halt as grit got into its bearings. Engineers took over a year to work out how to replace the bearings!

Combine Harvesters

When harvest time comes each year, wheat fields around the world begin to throb with the sound of giant machines called combine harvesters. Their task is to cut down the ripe wheat and gather the grain to make the flour we need for our bread. The world's biggest combine harvester, the Lexion 780, can gather over 700 tons of grain in a day—enough to make nearly a million loaves!

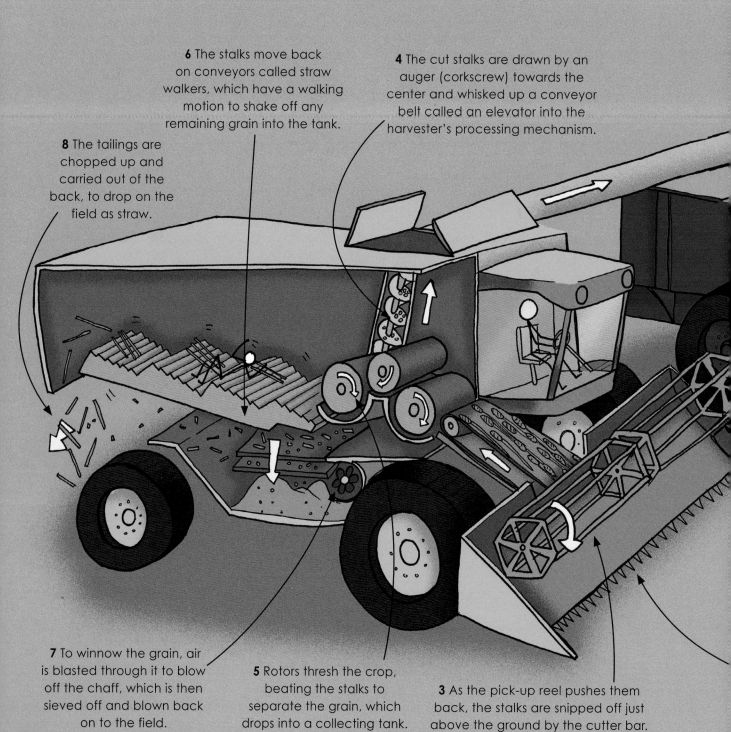

6 The stalks move back on conveyors called straw walkers, which have a walking motion to shake off any remaining grain into the tank.

4 The cut stalks are drawn by an auger (corkscrew) towards the center and whisked up a conveyor belt called an elevator into the harvester's processing mechanism.

8 The tailings are chopped up and carried out of the back, to drop on the field as straw.

7 To winnow the grain, air is blasted through it to blow off the chaff, which is then sieved off and blown back on to the field.

5 Rotors thresh the crop, beating the stalks to separate the grain, which drops into a collecting tank.

3 As the pick-up reel pushes them back, the stalks are snipped off just above the ground by the cutter bar.

All-in-One Harvesters

Combine harvesters get their name from combining all the tasks needed to gather wheat. As they drive through a field of ripe wheat or any other cereal crop, they cut the stalks, separate the grain, and clean and collect it automatically, using rotating blades, wheels, sieves, and conveyors. They combine the three main tasks in harvesting:

- Reaping—cutting and gathering the stalks

- Threshing—shaking or beating the stalks to loosen the grain from the tailings, the stalks that become straw

- Winnowing—getting rid of the scaly unwanted chaff, which holds the grain

9 When the grain tank is full, the grain is carried up from the tank by an elevator and shoots out of a side pipe (sometimes called the unloader) into a waiting trailer.

Tiring Work

Hefty farm machines have to cross soft earth and mud in all kinds of terrain and weather. They have some of the biggest, chunkiest tires in the world. The biggest tractor tires are almost 9 ft (2.7 m) tall.

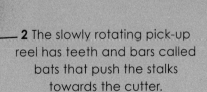

2 The slowly rotating pick-up reel has teeth and bars called bats that push the stalks towards the cutter.

1 The header gathers the stalks in at the front with a pair of sharp pincers called crop dividers.

Semisubmersible Rigs

Some of the best sources of oil and natural gas lie below the seabed. To get at them, oil rig workers have to set up huge drilling platforms out at sea. But what if the water is too deep to rest the supports for the platform on the seabed? Then what's needed is a semisubmersible rig, which rests on pontoons (tanks) that float just under the surface of the sea.

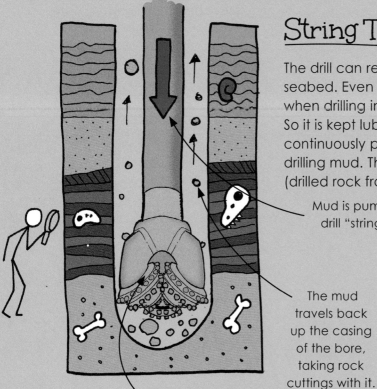

A nozzle sprays mud on to the drill bit, cleaning the bit in the process.

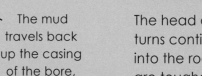

The mud travels back up the casing of the bore, taking rock cuttings with it.

String Time

The drill can reach 20,000 ft (7,000 m) into the seabed. Even under the sea, it could overheat when drilling into the solid rock of the seabed. So it is kept lubricated, cooled, and cleaned by continuously pumping in a special fluid called drilling mud. The mud also brings the cuttings (drilled rock fragments) up to the surface.

Mud is pumped down inside the drill "string"—its entire length

Tough Bits

The head of the drill, or drill bit, turns continuously and cuts slowly into the rock. Its cutting edges are toughened with different materials according to the rock type. Such materials include steel, tungsten-carbide, PDC (synthetic diamond), or even real diamond.

Gusher!

Once the hole has been drilled, the oil has to be extracted. So the rig workers reinforce the newly drilled hole with a casing of concrete. Next, they make little holes in the casing near the bottom to let oil in, and top the well with a "Christmas tree" of control valves. Finally, they send down acid or pressurized sand to break through the last layer of rock. The oil then gushes up through the pipe under its own pressure.

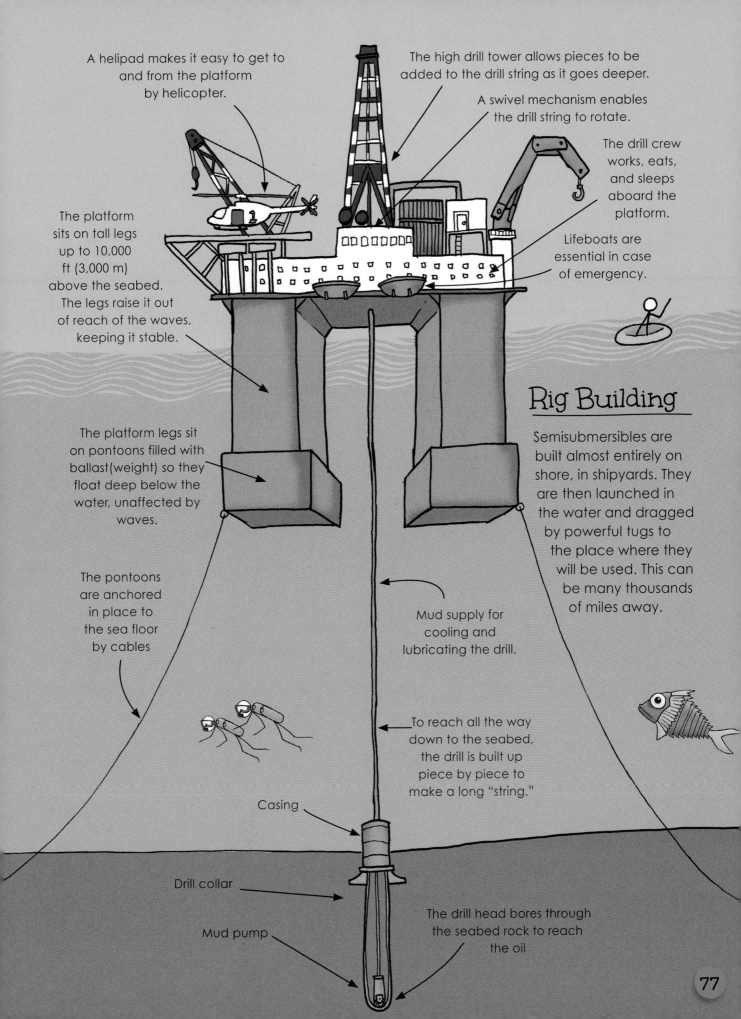

A helipad makes it easy to get to and from the platform by helicopter.

The high drill tower allows pieces to be added to the drill string as it goes deeper.

A swivel mechanism enables the drill string to rotate.

The drill crew works, eats, and sleeps aboard the platform.

The platform sits on tall legs up to 10,000 ft (3,000 m) above the seabed. The legs raise it out of reach of the waves, keeping it stable.

Lifeboats are essential in case of emergency.

The platform legs sit on pontoons filled with ballast(weight) so they float deep below the water, unaffected by waves.

Rig Building

Semisubmersibles are built almost entirely on shore, in shipyards. They are then launched in the water and dragged by powerful tugs to the place where they will be used. This can be many thousands of miles away.

The pontoons are anchored in place to the sea floor by cables

Mud supply for cooling and lubricating the drill.

To reach all the way down to the seabed, the drill is built up piece by piece to make a long "string."

Casing

Drill collar

The drill head bores through the seabed rock to reach the oil

Mud pump

The top of the first hill is the highest point of the ride. So it has maximum potential energy. From this point, it can only go downhill . . . or can it?

Wheels All Around

A roller coaster needs special wheels to hold it to the track as it roars from side to side and even goes upside down. Ordinary train wheels can run only on top of the track. But roller-coaster wheels must run on top, along the side and underneath too.

When you zoom down the slopes, you go into free fall and float off the seat, apparently weightless.

As the cars hurtle faster and faster down the first slope, they gain kinetic energy— the energy of motion.

After whizzing down the first hill, the cars have huge momentum. This means they are so loaded with kinetic energy they can zoom right up again—either high up another hill or around in a loop.

⇨ = acceleration

➡ = centrifugal force

➡ = gravity

Loop the Loop

As they loop, cars are held on to the track by the "apparent force" created by the tug-of-war between gravity and the changing direction of their own acceleration. Loops on roller coasters have to be teardrop-shaped, not round, to keep the forces in balance.

Roller Coasters

Roller coasters might look like very mad trains. But these super-scary rides need no engine or power. They are driven by gravity and momentum alone. They only need power to launch them from the top of the first hill. After that, they just go and go . . .

Liftoff

On older roller coasters, the ride starts with a slow haul up the first, tallest hill (called the lift hill) by a chain that hooks into the base of the cars. As the train climbs higher, the farther it has to fall, and the more potential energy it gains—the energy of gravity.

Whoosh!

Instead of the slow crawl up the lift hill, modern roller coasters start with a power launch that blasts you straight to high speeds, using electromagnets, hydraulics, or compressed air. Within a few seconds of the start you may be traveling at 100 mph (160 km/h)!

Shooting down the big loop, they gain enough kinetic energy to roar up the second loop. They've lost a bit of energy, though, so the second loop has to be smaller.

Climbing to the top of the second loop gives another boost in potential energy— enough to make the cars accelerate again.

The acceleration is just enough to give the cars the kinetic energy to climb the final slope, even though friction and air resistance begin to slow them down.

The cars are brought to a halt at the end by magnetic brakes.

Older roller coasters have wooden tracks, but most modern tracks are tubes of steel that can be twisted into all kinds of shapes.

Safety is vital on roller coasters, so riders are strapped or barred in securely before the ride.

Large Hadron Collider

The best way to find out what atoms are made of is to smash them together so they break apart. To do this, scientists build giant machines called particle accelerators in deep tunnels. Here, powerful magnets accelerate particles to huge speeds and hurl them together. The Large Hadron Collider (LHC) is the biggest.

Electromagnet coil

Inner detectors

Heat detectors

Muon detectors

The Detectors

Around the ring there are six detectors where scientists can make observations and perform experiments. They are a bit like digital cameras. Although the particles they study are tiny, the detectors can be as much as three storys high and weigh more than 5,000 tons. The biggest is ATLAS. It is so big and complicated it had to be taken underground in pieces and took five years to assemble. Its task is to detect collisions between protons.

Giant Research Project

The LHC is located deep underground on the border between Switzerland and France. It is run by CERN, the European Organization for Nuclear Research.

The Higgs Boson

The LHC has become famous for its hunt for a special particle called the Higgs Boson. It is this mysterious particle that scientists think may explain why things have mass—that is, why some things are light and others heavy. In 2013, they confirmed that they had seen it in the LHC, but no one knows quite what that means yet.

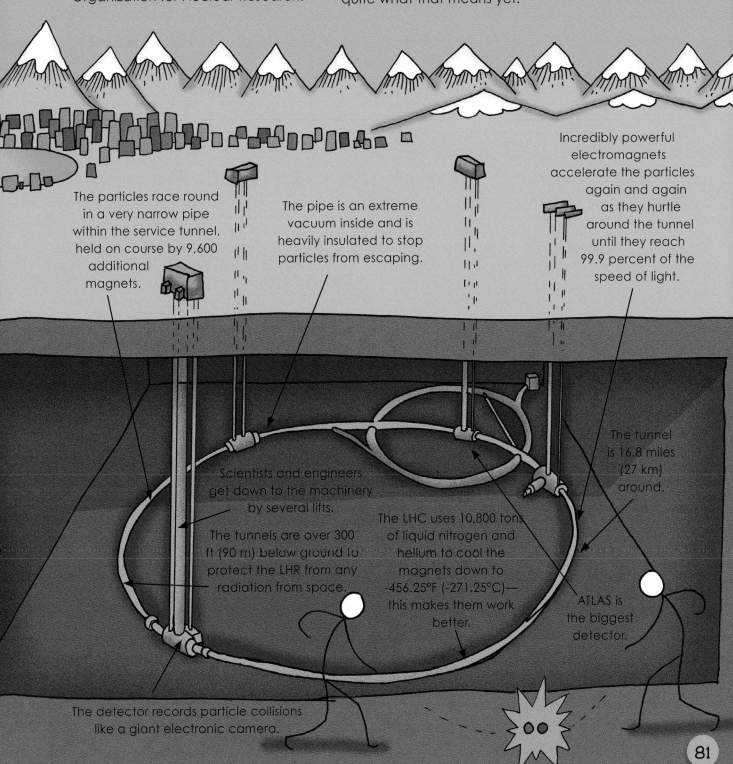

The particles race round in a very narrow pipe within the service tunnel, held on course by 9,600 additional magnets.

The pipe is an extreme vacuum inside and is heavily insulated to stop particles from escaping.

Incredibly powerful electromagnets accelerate the particles again and again as they hurtle around the tunnel until they reach 99.9 percent of the speed of light.

Scientists and engineers get down to the machinery by several lifts.

The tunnels are over 300 ft (90 m) below ground to protect the LHR from any radiation from space.

The LHC uses 10,800 tons of liquid nitrogen and helium to cool the magnets down to -456.25°F (-271.25°C)— this makes them work better.

The tunnel is 16.8 miles (27 km) around.

ATLAS is the biggest detector.

The detector records particle collisions like a giant electronic camera.

Control Room

When moving a spacecraft as tall as a skyscraper, the crew have to keep the platform level. The top of the spacecraft cannot be out of vertical by even a fraction. In the control room, they check the level constantly with laser and electronic technology and make adjustments with the JEL (Jacking, Equalization, and Leveling) system.

There is a driver's cab at each corner: two for when the crawler is going backwards and two for when it's moving forward.

The four generators provide electric power for the 16 traction motors that drive the wheels.

Originally, the crawlers could carry a staggering 7,000-ton load, but they have recently been upgraded to take over 9,000 tons.

The crawler is operated by a team of 30 engineers, technicians and drivers.

The crawler's flat top allows it to slide under the launch platform to pick up the entire platform and tower, along with its spacecraft load.

3

Two giant diesel engines, each generating 2,750 horsepower, drive the four electricity generators, one for each track unit.

Crawler Vehicles

Hans and Franz are the crawler vehicles used at the Kennedy Space Center in the US. Their task is to carry spacecraft from the buildings where they are assembled to the launchpads, ready to be blasted into space. They are the world's biggest self-propelled vehicles. Bucket wheel excavators may be bigger, but only Hans and Franz can move under their own power.

What Do They Carry?

- The crawlers were originally built to move the giant Saturn V rockets that carried the Apollo moon missions. That meant they were carrying a rocket that was 363 ft (110 m) tall, as well as its 398-ft (121-m) launch tower.

- After the Apollo missions finished, from 1979 the crawlers were reused for over 30 years to carry the shuttles and their boosters into place for launch.

- Revamped, one crawler will take commercial rockets to the launchpad, while the other will carry the 320-ft (97.5-m) Space Launch System designed to launch missions to Mars.

The crawlers are 131 ft (40 m) long and 113 ft (34 m) wide.

The height of the crawler can be altered from 20 ft (6 m) to 26 ft (8 m).

Jacking cylinders can raise each side independently by up to 1.8 m (6 ft) to keep the platform completely level.

The track units can swivel independently to steer the crawler.

The crawler runs on four track units, each with two tracks, and each powered by four electric motors.

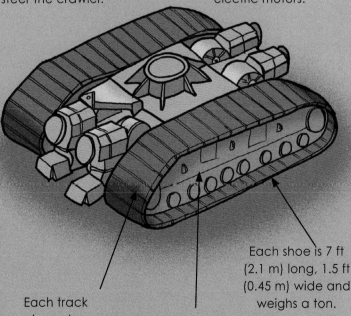

The crawlers can reach a speed of 1 mph (1.6 km/h) loaded and 2 mph (3.2 km/h) unloaded.

The crawler weighs 2,750 tons without a load.

Each track is made from 57 steel shoes.

The wheels run round inside their own moving track, which spreads the load.

Each shoe is 7 ft (2.1 m) long, 1.5 ft (0.45 m) wide and weighs a ton.

Strange Inventions

Wacky design ideas for cars, bikes, and trains date back centuries.

Heroic Steam

You may think steam power is only a few hundred years old. Think again. About 2,000 years ago, a Greek inventor aptly called Hero (of Alexandria in Egypt) built an amazing device called a wind bal,l or aeolipile. It was a round kettle that could be set spinning on a pivot by jets of steam gushing from nozzles on either side. Hero was even more ahead of his time than you might think: it's not just a steam engine, it's a jet engine. But Hero hadn't a clue what to do with it...

The Wheel Thing

In 1930, John Archibald Purves of Somerset in England decided to do away with three of a car's wheels and manage with just one. But it was a big one! Driver and passenger sat inside the wheel, and the engine turned the wheel by trying to climb up the inside. Several models were built and they could reach 30 mph. The only problem was steering . . . and stopping.

Water Wheels

Steam-engine pioneer Oliver Evans of Delaware was nothing if not inventive. When he built the world's first steam-powered dredging machine in 1805, he realized it wouldn't be much use if he couldn't get it to the river. So he gave his machine wheels and created America's first car—and the world's first amphibious car. He even gave it the suitably weird name Oruktor Amphibolos.

RocketSkates

Who needs a car or a motorcycle or a train when you've got motorized shoes? Los Angeles designer Peter Treadway came up with the idea of making battery-powered, motorized shoes that strap on your normal pair. You simply shift their weight forward to accelerate and backwards to slow down. They move at up to 12 mph and cover 6-10 miles before the batteries need recharging.

Sparks of Invention

Thomas Davenport of Williamstown, Vermont, was stunned when he saw the world's first powerful electromagnet lifting metal in 1831. Right away, he realized the power of electromagnetism to turn as well as pull and created an early electric motor. And just a few years later, in 1835, he created the world's first electric car. Sadly, batteries in those days were useless, so it wasn't very practical.

Magic Doors

If you thought automatic doors were pretty modern, think again. Nearly 2,000 years ago, a mechanical genius called Hero, who lived in Alexandria in Egypt, invented a mechanism for opening the gigantic doors of Greek temples as if by magic. When the priests lit a fire on the altar, the hot air was used to move water, which then triggered an ingenious mechanism to move counterweights that swung the great doors open—and even blew hot air to create a blast on giant trumpets. No wonder visitors were awed.

Giant Wood Ant

It looks like a terrifying six-legged giant insect. In fact, the "walking harvester" by Plustech/Timberjack was the prototype for a real machine designed to help lumberjacks cut and gather trees in tricky terrain. The legs are moved in an ant-like way by computer according to the driver's instructions. It has an antenna-like arm at the front for chopping down trees and picking them up.

Cosmic Clock

Robots may seem like recent creations—but inventors have been designing automata (machines that work by themselves) for thousands of years. One of the biggest was the Cosmic Engine of Chinese minister Su Sung. This was actually one of the first clocks. It was 30 ft (9 m) high and worked via rotating wheels and water pressure (or liquid mercury). At certain times of day, full-sized mechanical men and women at the top would ring bells and bash gongs. It ran for 30 years between 1092 and 1126CE.

Fountain Machine

King Louis XIV of France wanted the world's biggest fountains to shoot water into the air at his palace at Versailles. So he commissioned the Marly Machine, finished in 1684. This huge pumping machine, with its 250 pumps, used an array of giant paddles to force water 500 ft (152 m) up from the River Seine to the palace gardens. It pumped as much water every day as was consumed by the entire population of Paris.

The World's Biggest Spider

In 2008, French company La Machine presented their giant mechanical spider—just for fun—at a parade in Liverpool, UK, as part of the city's celebrations as European capital of culture. The towering arachnid, nicknamed La Princesse, is 50 ft (15 m) tall and weighs 37 tons. It walks on eight legs with 50 hydraulically moved joints, and it needs 12 people to operate it.

People have had crazy ideas for watercraft for very many years . . .

Who Needs Oars or Sails?

Mechanically powered boats are nothing new. Back in the Middle Ages, numerous inventors came up with ideas for paddle-driven boats. One manuscript from that period shows a boat with multiple paddles, and animals such as cows providing the power to turn the paddles. And in one book from Roman times, there is an illustration of an ox-driven paddle boat.

Water Bike

Who said you can't ride your bike across the sea? A water bike is a boat made by simply attaching a bicycle to floats and the pedals to paddles that drive it along. San Francisco inventor Judah Schiller created a water bike called the BayCycle— and in 2013 became the first person to cross San Francisco Bay on a bicycle.

Wavecutter

Earthrace looked more like a giant cartoon crow than a boat. It was a trimaran—a boat with three hulls. With its long sharp nose, it was meant to slice straight through waves rather than ride over the top. The idea was to break the round-the-world speed record for a power boat, but technical problems interrupted the record attempt. It was renamed Ady Gil became involved in protests against whaling—and was then sunk by a Japanese whaling ship.

Dolphin Boat

The Innespace Seabreacher has got to be one of the most extraordinary submarines ever. It's a tiny one-person sub shaped just like a dolphin that is powered like a jet ski and is completely acrobatic. As well as whizzing over the water at speeds of more than 40 mph (65 km/h), it can dive, roll, and even jump right out of the water just like a live dolphin.

Look, Wave-walker

The WAM-V, or Wave Adaptive Modular Vessel, looks like something from a *Star Wars* movie. It skims along on two giant inflatable tubes that independently dance up and down over the waves. That way the passengers, carried high above in a gondola, itself supported on spider-like legs, stay rock-steady and only the tubes move, like giant feet.

Wacky designs for flying machines from the last century (and before) . . .

The Plane for Rain?

Who said an aircraft has to have two long wings? New York inventor William Romme didn't think so. With the help of Chance Vought he built the Cycloplane in Chicago. It came to be called the Umbrella Plane because its fabric wings were stretched over spokes just like an umbrella. Amazingly, it actually flew a number of times between 1911 and 1913.

In a Flap

Countless inventors have been inspired by the birds to build aircraft with flapping wings. Aircraft like this are called ornithopters. The first was designed by the 15th-century Italian genius Leonardo da Vinci. One of the more successful was George White's pedal-powered ornithopter which flew almost a mile along St Augustine Beach in Florida in 1928. People are still trying to build ornithopters even now.

Flying Saucer

Who said flying saucers come from outer space? In the 1950s, the US military and Avro Canada teamed up to build one in secret. They named it the Avrocar, though some called it the Silver Bug. It lifted off using the downdraught from a powerful turbofan in the middle. It only flew at 35 mph (56 km/h) and hovered just a few feet off the ground. But Avro engineers thought it might fly at 300 mph (480 km/h) and reach 10,000 ft (3,048 m).

Sea Skimmer

Russian engineer Rostislav Alexeyev realized there was no need for planes to fly high. If they flew just above the surface of the Earth, they experienced a bonus lift known as the ground effect. In the 1980s, his team developed the Lun-class Ekranoplan Ground Effect Vehicle. This was a giant sea plane more than 200 ft (60 m) long that skimmed just 12 ft (3.6 m) above the surface of the sea and yet remained undetected by radar.

Wing ding ring

The earliest planes had not just one pair of wings, but often two (biplanes) or even three (triplanes). In 1907, a French navy engineer, the Marquis d'Equevilly, built his 'Multiplane' with five pairs of half wings and two full wings—all enclosed in a pair of hoops. The next year, he built another version with 50 wings!

Glossary

aerofoil

Special shape of an aircraft wing, with a curved surface that provides lift

aileron

Hinged flap on the outside edge of the wing that allows the plane to roll to one side or the other

altimeter

Instrument that tells the pilot how high the plane is flying

autopilot

System for controlling the aircraft automatically without the pilot's input

bank

Airplane turn in which the plane tilts at an angle as it turns

bilge

The bottom of the inside of the hull

bogie

The frame beneath a railroad truck or carriage holding the wheels and axles

bow

The front of the boat

bridge

The place on a large ship from where it is controlled

camshaft

A rod with a row of egg-shaped lobes that open the engine valves as they turn

catalytic converter

Box that filters some of the polluting gases out of car exhausts, using a chemical catalyst

catamaran

A boat with two linked hulls side by side

chine

The bend in a hull profile

cockpit

The place where the pilot and copilot sit

collective pitch

The angle of all the rotor blades of a helicopter

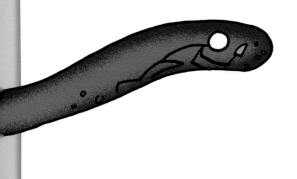

crankshaft

A specially-shaped rod in an engine that turns the up and down movement of the pistons into a circular motion

cutterhead

The cutting face of a tunnel boring machine

cyclic pitch

When the rotor blades of a helicopter change pitch at a particular part of their rotation

cylinder

The tube in an engine in which the fuel is ignited to push down the pistons

shock absorber

An oil-filled tube, also known as a shock-absorber, that slows down, or dampens, the bouncing of the suspension springs

electromagnets

Powerful magnets activated by an electric current

elevator

Hinged flap on the rear wings that controls the pitch of an aircraft

flap

Hinged surface on the outside edge of the wing that controls the lift and speed of the plane

fuselage

The central body of an aircraft

hadron

Any particle, such as protons and neutrons, made with a combination of quarks, the most basic particles of all

haul truck

A giant dump truck used in mines and quarrie

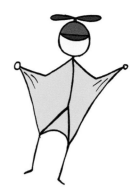

helm

The steering of a ship

hopper

An open container for loose bulk material that can be1 easily tipped or poured out

hull

The watertight body shell of a boat

hybrid

A vehicle that combines technologies, typically a vehicle that uses an electric motor with a gasoline or diesel engine

hydraulic

Power system based on pushing fluids through tubes with pistons

hydrofoil

A boat that rides up out of the water on wing-like foils on legs

jib

The long arm that carries a crane's load

joystick

The handle that the pilot uses to control the plane by moving wing flaps

keel

The fin or backbone of a boat

kinetic energy

The energy something has because it is moving

live rail

A rail carrying an electric current that an electric locomotive can pick up to power its motor

pantograph

The flexible arm that an electric locomotive uses to pick up electric power from an overhead cable

pilot

Expert who guides a ship

piston

The drum that plugs the cylinder in an engine and is pushed down when fuel is ignited, so turning the crankshaft

pitch

The tilt of the plane from back to front

port

The left of the ship, going forward

potential energy

The energy something has because of its position, typically its height above the ground

reaping

Cutting and gathering the stalks when harvesting cereals

rigging

The ropes and wires that hold masts and sails up on a sailing ship

rudder

The hinged steering blade that projects from the stern of the boat

slewing unit

The turntable at the top of the crane tower that allows the jib to swivel

solar cell

Unit that converts sunlight to electricity, also known as a photo-voltaic cell

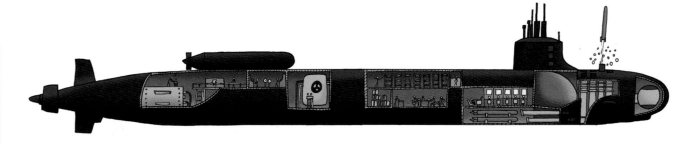

spark plug

A small device that ignites fuel in an engine's cylinder as an electric spark leaps across a gap

starboard

The right of the ship, going forward

stern

The back end of a boat

submersible

A craft or machine designed to work underwater

threshing

Shaking or beating the stalks to loosen the grain when harvesting cereals

tiller

A long hinged arm for controlling the rudder

torque

The turning force of an engine

tower crane

A crane on a tall tower

trimaran

A boat with three linked hulls side by side

turbine

Powerful engine that works by using pressurized gases to turn a fan blade

turbofan

Jet engine that runs more quietly by using an extra fan to provide a bypass of cool air

turboprop

Jet engine that uses the jet thrust to turn a propeller

winnowing

Getting rid of scaly unwanted chaff, which holds the grain, when harvesting cereals

yaw

When the plane steers one way or the other without banking

INDEX

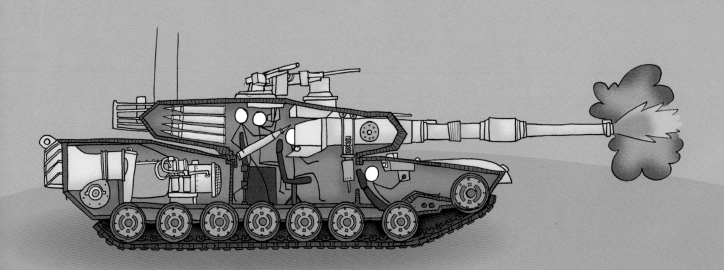

The Author

John Farndon is Royal Literary Fellow at Anglia Ruskin University in Cambridge, UK. He has written numerous books for adults and children on science, technology, and nature and been shortlisted four times for the Royal Society's Young People's Book Prize. He has recently been creating science stories for children for the Moscow Polytech science festival.

The Illustrator

John Paul has a BSc in Biology from the University of Sussex, UK, and a graduate certificate in animation from the University of the West of England. He devotes his spare time to growing chilli peppers, perfecting his plan for a sustainable future, and caring for a small plastic dinosaur. He has three pet squid that live in the bath, which makes drawing in ink quite economical.

Picture Credits (abbreviations: t = top; b = bottom; c = center; l = left; r = right)
© www.shutterstock.com: 6 tr, 7 tr, 7 bl, 8 tl, 8 cr, 8 b, 9 tl, 9 tr, 9 c, 9 br. 6 bl Jorg Hackemann / Shutterstock.com, 7cl Jorg Hackemann / Shutterstock.com, 7 cr Kijja Pruchyathamkorn / Shutterstock.com. 8 cl Irina Rogova / Shutterstock.com, 8tr Irina Rogova / Shutterstock.com, 9bl Kuznetsov Viktor / Shutterstock.com, 9 br Takamex / Shutterstock.com
Every effort has been taken to trace the copyright holder. And we acknowldge in advance any unintentional ommissions.
We would be pleased to insert the appropriate acknowledgement in any subsequent edition of this publication.